ORTHO'S All About

The Easiest Roses To Grow

Written by
Dr. Tommy Cairns, President, American Rose Society

Meredith® Books
Des Moines, Iowa

Ortho® Books
An imprint of Meredith® Books

All About The Easiest Roses to Grow
Editor: Michael McKinley
Contributing Editors: David Haupert, Penelope O'Sullivan
Contributing Technical Editors: Tom Carruth, Anne
   Graber, Steve Hutton, Keith Zary
Senior Associate Design Director: Tom Wegner
Assistant Editor: Harijs Priekulis
Copy Chief: Terri Fredrickson
Editorial Operations Manager: Karen Schirm
Managers, Book Production: Pam Kvitne,
   Marjorie J. Schenkelberg
Contributing Copy Editor: Barbara Feller-Roth
Technical Proofreader: Fran Gardner
Contributing Proofreaders: Beth Lastine, Ginny Perrin,
   Barbara J. Stokes, Jo Ellyn Witke
Contributing Map Illustrator: Jana Fothergill
Indexer: Ellen Davenport
Electronic Production Coordinator: Paula Forest
Editorial and Design Assistant: Kathleen Stevens

Additional Editorial Contributions from
   Art Rep Services
Director: Chip Nadeau
Designers: lk Design
Illustrator: Glory Bechtold

Meredith® Books
Editor in Chief: James D. Blume
Design Director: Matt Strelecki
Managing Editor: Gregory H. Kayko
Executive Editor, Gardening and Home Improvement:
   Benjamin W. Allen

Director, Sales, Special Markets: Rita McMullen
Director, Sales, Premiums: Michael A. Peterson
Director, Sales, Retail: Tom Wierzbicki
Director, Book Marketing: Brad Elmitt
Director, Operations: George A. Susral
Director, Production: Douglas M. Johnston

Meredith Publishing Group
President, Publishing Group: Stephen M. Lacy

Meredith Corporation
Chairman and Chief Executive Officer: William T. Kerr
Chairman of the Executive Committee: E.T. Meredith III

Thanks to
Janet Anderson, Studio Au, Rosemary A. Kautzky, Sandra
Neff, and Spectrum Communications Services. Thanks also
to the following people and organizations for providing
assistance and locations for photography: Dr. Tommy Cairns
and Luis Desamero, Lillian Ruth Berkowitz, Stan Zajdel,
Elvin McDonald, Rose Hills Memorial Gardens, Inc., at
Whittier, California, Daryl Johnson and the International
Rose Gardens of the City of Portland, Oregon, Clair G.
Martin III and the Huntington Library and Botanical
Gardens at San Marino, California, and Clare LaBerge and
the Montreal Botanical Garden.

Photographers
   (Photographers credited may retain copyright ©
   to the listed photographs.)
L = Left, R = Right, C = Center, B = Bottom, T = Top

Rich Baer: 33B, 47C, 75TR, 75B, 75Bi, 79C; **Laurie Black:**
15; **Karen Bussolini/Positive Images:** 13C; **John Elsley:**
9TR, 9TC, 21R, 43B; **Derek Fell:** 8B, 9TL, 11TCL, 10BR,
70; **John Glover:** 53B; **Jerry Harpur:** 11BL, 11TL, 21L,
82C, 82R; **Marcus Harpur:** 52BR; **Saxon Holt:** 8TR,
11BLC, 10BL, 13B, 17C, 17B, 20BR, 34B, 52L, 71B, 72T,
74L; **J&P™roses presented by Jackson & Perkins
Wholesale, Inc.:** 41B, 51TR; **Kathy Longinacker:** 16, 17T;
Janet Loughrey: 3, 5, 11TR; **Michael McKinley:** 3B, 4, 6,
7, 8TL, 8BL, 9BR, 9BL, 9C, 10TL, 10CR, 11RC, 11BR,
20T, 20BL, 22, 23, 24, 25, 26, 27, 28, 29, 30, 31, 32, 33T,
34T, 35, 36R, 37T, 37B, 38, 39, 40, 41T, 42R, 43T, 43C,
44, 45, 46, 47B, 48, 49T, 49C, 50, 51TL , 51B, 54, 55, 56,
57T, 57C, 59LC, 59RC, 59RC(i), 59B, 60, 61, 62, 63, 64,
65, 66, 67, 68, 69, 73, 74R, 75L, 76, 77T, 77C, 78, 79T,
79B, 80, 81, 82T, 83; **Ben Phillips/Positive Images:** 57B;
Sequoia Nursery: 71C, 72BR; **Richard Shiell:** 8CR, 10TR,
13T, 37C, 49B, 58, 59TR, 77B; **Albert Squillace/Positive
Images:** 3, 12; **Michael Thompson:** 8C, 36L, 52T, 53T,
71T, 72BL; **Weeks Roses:** 42L, 47T;

Cover photo: Janet Loughrey

All of us at Ortho® Books are dedicated to providing you
with the information and ideas you need to enhance your
home and garden. We welcome your comments and
suggestions about this book. Write to us at:
   Meredith Corporation
   Ortho Gardening Books
   1716 Locust St.
   Des Moines, IA 50309–3023

If you would like to purchase any of our gardening, home
improvement, cooking, crafts, or home decorating and
design books, check wherever quality books are sold. Or visit
us at: meredithbooks.com

If you would like more information on other Ortho
products, call 800-225-2883 or visit us at: www.ortho.com

Roses for Every Garden

Whether they're old-fashioned or modern, an abundance of roses is essential for any cottage garden. In this one, splashes of cottage pinks, bearded iris, and Jupiter's beard extend and emphasize the roses' message of luxuriant color.

Long recognized as America's favorite flower for hobby gardeners and floral arrangers, the rose is fast becoming America's favorite landscape plant too—and for good reason: No other single genus of flowering shrubs offers such diversity of form and hardworking color. Roses range from miniature 8-inch mounds to giant 40-foot climbers, and from sprawling ground covers to narrow vertical "trees." Roses can surround yards as hedges, fill wide beds, scramble up tall trellises, and spill out of window boxes. And the color! Roses are the very definition of flower power, available in nearly every hue. Some old garden roses burst forth in one massive two-week show in late spring. Many modern roses repeat this display again and again all summer for the longest,

most abundant, and most continuous bloom season of any flowering shrub.

The best news for landscaping with roses is that recent breeding efforts are creating a revolutionary new generation of roses with excellent disease resistance, attractive habit, low-maintenance needs, and summer-long blooms. These fuss-free, no-fear roses are the focus of this book. Many featured varieties are exciting new introductions. Some are classics that have withstood the test of time. Each rose has been selected because it excels in at least five of the following six criteria:

■ 1. It blooms all summer long with abundant flowers of good form, color, and fragrance.

■ 2. Its form and foliage are attractive.

■ 3. It has good resistance to black spot, powdery mildew, and rust.

■ 4. It is climate-hardy and can withstand severe winters and summer heat.

■ 5. It needs minimal deadheading, grooming, and pruning during the growing season.

■ 6. It is readily available throughout North America.

Whether you are an experienced rose grower who wants to learn more about the exciting new high-performance roses or someone who has always wanted to grow roses but has feared their sometimes daunting reputation, the easiest roses to grow open an entirely new world of gardening possibilities.

How to Use This Book

Selecting the right rose for the purpose and giving it the ideal conditions for healthy growth are two keys to success with roses. The rest of this section (pages 6–11) introduces, through photographs, the astonishing variety of flower colors and plant forms found in the easiest roses to grow—and the wide range of landscape roles these plants play. In "Success the Easy Way" (pages 12–19), techniques for purchasing, planting, and caring for roses are condensed into eight pages.

Most of the remainder of this book (pages 20–83) presents a selection guide to the easiest roses to grow, organized primarily by landscape function. Each spread features in photographs and descriptions the four or five easiest roses in a category, or that solve a particular landscape problem. Each spread also offers a list of additional recommended varieties. Because one exceptional rose may excel in several functions, it may appear more than once throughout the book.

Each rose is listed in this book with certain standard information. The varietal names used in this book are the ones most likely to be encountered in nurseries and catalogues. Capitalized names enclosed in single quotation marks are officially registered cultivar names. Capitalized names not enclosed in single quotation marks are commercial names, many of which are trademarked or registered. Each time a rose is listed in this book, its name is followed by its form (see pages 8–9), color category (see page 7), year of introduction, introducer or breeder, and, if applicable, important awards (see pages 28-29). The hardiness zones listed are from the USDA Plant Hardiness Zone Map (see page 92). The sizes listed are the average for that variety under optimum conditions.

While the roses presented in this book are the easiest to grow in North America, no rose is ever completely problem-free. Learning to recognize and solve problems before they become serious will help you to enjoy the rewards of roses with the least fuss. "The Ortho Rose Problem Solver" offered at the conclusion of this book (pages 84–90) condenses into a few handy pages all of the information pertinent to roses from the professional reference encyclopedia, *The Ortho Problem Solver*.

Roses are so versatile and diverse that you'll find just what you need to create virtually any landscape effect.

ANATOMY OF THE ROSE

Knowing the parts of a rose makes its cultivation easier. Starting from the ground up: A rose plant usually grows on an understock selected for its vigor. The named variety is grafted or budded onto the understock and grown for two years before it's harvested and sold to the public. The point of the original graft is called the bud union, or crown, from which flower-bearing canes emerge. These canes ensure the continued productivity and health of the plant.

Corolla is the technical term for the rose flower. Sepals, which drop down when the flower begins to bloom, protect the bud. The swollen part immediately under the flower is the calyx. The stem below the calyx is the peduncle. The reproductive organs, visible when the petals open, are in the center of the bloom.

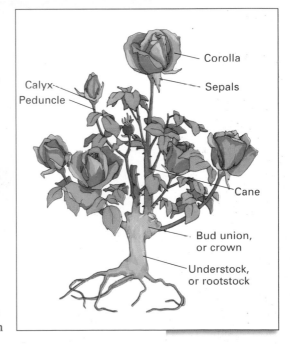

A World of Flowers

Through centuries of breeding the small, five-petalled, pink, white, or (rarely) yellow flowers of wild roses have proliferated into a vast selection of flower shapes, sizes, and colors.

BLOOM SHAPE

Rose blossoms have diverse shapes that range from broad, flat simplicity to high-centered sculptural elegance. Single-petaled varieties have a natural, "wild" charm, with flat, wide-open blooms and a central boss of stamens. The form of a many-petaled rose changes as it opens, usually exposing the central stamens. The blooms of some modern shrub roses and old garden roses are shaped like globes and rosettes, or organized in quarters. The hybrid tea shape is characterized by a high pointed center and symmetrically unfurling petals.

Flat ('Sally Holmes')

Classical high-centered ('Mister Lincoln')

Fully opened ('Frontier Twirl')

Globular (The Reeve)

Rosette (Sexy Rexy)

Quartered ('Sombreuil')

PETAL SHAPE

Most rose petals are plain and broad. Some are reflexed (with edges rolled under); ruffled (with undulating surfaces); and frilled (with pleated or serrated edges).

Broad (Bride's Dream)

Reflexed (Perfect Moment)

Ruffled ('Just Joey')

Frilled ('F.J. Grootendorst')

PETAL COUNT

The number of petals is a measure of the fullness of a flower. With roses, various terms are used to describe the petal count— as indicated in these examples—which ranges from 5 to more than 100.

Single: 5 to 12 petals (Pink Meidiland)

Semidouble: 13 to 16 petals (Rosa Mundi)

Double: 17 to 25 petals (Showbiz)

Full: 26 to 40 petals (Fragrant Cloud)

Very full: 41 and more petals (America)

ROSE COLORS

The astonishing range of colors offered by modern roses is unmatched by any other kind of flower. Except for true blue or black, there is a rose available in nearly every hue and shade. The American Rose Society, custodian of rose registrations, has developed the system of 18 official color classifications used in this book. The only classification not represented here is russet, a relatively rare color that is unavailable to date among the easiest roses to grow.

White, near white, and white blend (Irresistible)

Light yellow (Elina)

Medium yellow (Toulouse Lautrec)

Deep yellow (Goldmarie)

Yellow blend (Sheila's Perfume)

Apricot and apricot blend ('Loving Touch')

Orange and orange blend (Livin' Easy)

Orange-pink and orange-pink blend (All That Jazz)

Orange-red and orange-red blend (Paprika)

Light pink ('Royal Highness')

Medium pink ('Queen Elizabeth')

Deep pink ('William Baffin')

Pink blend (Gemini)

Medium red (Olympiad)

Dark red (The Prince)

Red blend (Handel)

Mauve and mauve blend (Intrigue)

FLOWER COLOR PATTERNS

Patterns not shown here include picotee (contrasting petal edge) and bicolor (petal front and back in different hues).

Solid (Sun Flare)

Blushed or blended (Double Delight)

Striped (Scentimental)

Hand-painted (Brilliant Pink Iceberg)

Plants in All Shapes and Sizes

From tiny miniatures for flower pots to giant ramblers that can cover a house, roses possess a broader diversity of plant size and form than any other flowering shrub. Shown here are some of the official and commercial classifications used in this book to organize roses into distinct groups.

Shrub: *Wide diversity in flower form and size, and plant size. Flowers are often large (3 to 4 inches in diameter) on mound-shaped plants 4 to 6 feet tall. Above: All That Jazz.*

Hybrid Tea: *Perhaps the most popular class of modern roses, easily recognizable by the large, shapely, symmetrical 3- to 6-inch blooms containing 30 to 50 petals. Flowers are borne one to a stem. Because of their strong, vigorous canes, plants are usually upright, 4 to 7 feet tall, and leggy at the base. Above: St. Patrick.*

Grandiflora: *Similar to hybrid teas but with the added ability to bear clusters. Plants often grow to a commanding height of 6 to 8 feet tall, providing massive displays of blooms. Above: Crimson Bouquet.*

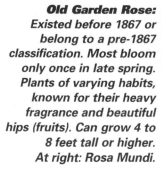

Miniature: *Flower form and foliage are miniature versions (blooms 1 to 2 inches in diameter) of hybrid teas and floribundas. Popularity of this class is due to its versatility for edging and growing in containers. Plants generally reach a height of 1 to 2 feet. Above: Glowing Amber.*

Floribunda: *Characterized by its profuse ability to bear 1- to 3-inch flowers in large clusters, or trusses. Matchless for providing massive, colorful, long-lasting garden displays. Bushes are often rounded mounds 3 to 4 feet tall. Above: Golden Border.*

Old Garden Rose: *Existed before 1867 or belong to a pre-1867 classification. Most bloom only once in late spring. Plants of varying habits, known for their heavy fragrance and beautiful hips (fruits). Can grow 4 to 8 feet tall or higher. At right: Rosa Mundi.*

Patio Tree: *For small rose plants such as miniatures, shrublets, and some floribundas, a tree height of 2 feet is used to create an effective display. Above: Gourmet Popcorn.*

Standard Tree: *Novel way of growing your favorite hybrid tea, floribunda, or miniature off the ground, grafted on a tall trunk from 3 to 5 feet high. Often used as formal accent. Above: Iceberg.*

Rambler: *Massive plants that can grow 30 feet in every direction to cover a tree or even a house. Flowers are small (about 1 to 2 inches wide), and some varieties have only one bloom cycle per season. Above:* Rosa banksiae lutea, *the Lady Banks rose.*

Shrublet: *Commercial description of a plant with general shrublike characteristics but a somewhat smaller stature, leaf, and flower. Flowers are usually 1 to 2 inches in diameter. At left: Pillow Fight.*

Ground Cover: *A new landscaping category of low-growing plants that spread in all directions up to 8 feet across to provide a carpet of color. Above: White Meidiland.*

Climber: *Growth habit is dominated by the production of long arching canes that can be trained to climb (if properly positioned and tied) on fences, walls, trellises, arbors, and pergolas. Above: 'Dortmund', trained against a wall.*

Roses in the Landscape

Roses offer a painter's palette of color in many forms and shapes. Although often grown in beds, roses lend themselves to a huge variety of landscape uses, from colorful hedges and ground covers to containerized accents for a patio and climbers to create a wall of spectacular hues. Many roses bloom all summer long, unlike many other flowers, and can complement a garden by providing color that continues long after other plants have finished blooming. Most of the roses in this book are seldom without flowers all summer.

The Formal Look *(see pages 74–75): Upright standard tree roses emphasize the geometric symmetry common to formal designs. Above: 'Mister Lincoln' standard tree roses.*

The Country Look *(see pages 48–57): For informal spontaneity and splash, intersperse with colorful companion plants.*

Eye-catching Beds and Edging *(see pages 42–43, 46–47): A single variety can make a powerful statement when massed. Above: Knock Out and the miniature, Child's Play.*

Hedges *(see pages 44–45): Instead of erecting a plain fence, plant roses to form a living one. They quickly create a thorny barrier even your pet cannot penetrate. At left: Simplicity, one of the first shrub roses bred specifically to perform well as a hedge.*

Covering Fences *(see pages 58–59): Climbers and ramblers do a good job of adding charm and color to any fence. Climbing roses reach a height and width of 4 to 20 feet; ramblers can spread 20 to 30 feet in any direction. Above: the classic duo of 'Blaze Improved' (a large-flowered climber) and a white rail fence.*

Adding Height *(see pages 60–65): Because most climbers bloom best when their canes are horizontal, not all flower on a pillar. But pillar roses do bloom freely when trained on a vertical plane. At near right: 'Zephirine Drouhin'.*

For arbors, choose roses that flower from ground level to the tips of their long canes. At far right: 'Lavender Lassie'. Small climbers add color on low walls and fences. At near right: 'Jeanne LaJoie'.

Filling Small Spaces *(see pages 68–75): Some roses don't need a lot of space to look their best. Miniature or mini-flora roses can add color and charm. At top left is the miniature Rainbow's End.*

Covering the Ground *(see pages 40–41): Use low-growing, spreading roses to cover garden areas and stabilize slopes. They require no maintenance because they are disease-resistant and self-cleaning. Above: Cliffs of Dover will spread to create a dense cover. Below: When planted above a wall, some ground-cover roses spill down beautifully over the edge, as does this* Rosa wichuraiana *'Poteriifolia'.*

For portable containers, use roses that stay narrow and upright or form dense, floral mounds. At left: Flower Carpet.

Success
The Easy Way

Water applied from above, like rain, can help discourage mites and aphids. Try to water early in the day so foliage can dry before nightfall.

Select from the easy roses featured in this book and you are well on your way to the greatest rewards for the least effort. However, even the easiest roses to grow need a three-part plan for ultimate success.

1. CHOOSE THE RIGHT ROSE FOR THE SITE. Select first for correct hardiness, size, and plant form. Then decide on color and bloom shape. All roses in this book are labeled with the USDA Hardiness Zones in which they are likely to survive winter without special protection. See page 92 to locate the hardiness zone in which you garden.

2. PLANT WHERE CONDITIONS ARE IDEAL. Roses need sunlight—at least six hours of it each day. Roses need good soil, rich in nutrients and organic matter, and moist but well-drained. And roses need adequate space for good air circulation (but not wind) in order to keep their foliage dry and to resist disease.

3. MAINTAIN VIGOR WITH FERTILIZER AND WATER. Gardeners demand a lot from easy roses—vigorous growth that resists pests and disease, and remarkable summer-long blooms. This high performance takes plenty of food and water. Plant roses well away from the roots of trees and other shrubs that might rob them of nutrients and moisture. And plan on a regular program of feeding and irrigation.

ROOM TO GROW

Besides providing good air circulation, adequate space around rose bushes permits you to fertilize and prune them properly when they are fully grown. Allow enough room so that you can access the center of the planting from at least one side. Consider the ultimate size of the plant. Hybrid teas and grandifloras should be planted 2 to 2½ feet apart (3 to 4 feet in Zones 7 through 10). Floribundas need less room, 1½ to 2 feet (2 to 3 feet apart in Zones 7 through 10). Plant miniatures 1 to 3 feet apart, depending on the variety and climate. Plant species, shrub, and old garden roses 5 to 6 feet apart (up to twice that distance in Zones 7 through 10).

SOIL TEXTURE AND STRUCTURE

Get to know your soil. Grab a handful of moist soil and squeeze it into a ball. When released, clay soil will stick together, sandy soil will fall apart, and silty soil will feel greasy. If the ball holds its shape but crumbles under a little finger-poking, you probably have sandy loam—the best soil for growing roses.

The texture is important because it affects how easily roots can absorb water and oxygen. Clay soils don't take in water well and when they are saturated, they won't release it. And because clay soils lack air spaces they can starve roots of necessary oxygen. Sandy soils drain too quickly, robbing the roots of moisture and nutrients. The proper soil for roses is a mix of sand, clay, and organic matter in proportions of roughly one-third each that strike the right balance between good drainage and nutrient and water retention.

ACIDITY AND ALKALINITY

Soil pH—a measure of its acidity and alkalinity—can also have a profound influence on the health of a rose. Soil pH is measured in a scale from 0 to 14. A value of 7 is neutral, below pH 7 is acidic, and above pH 7 is alkaline. Soil pH is important because it affects the rate at which plants absorb nutrients. Roses grow well in soils that are within a pH range of 5.8 to 6.8. You can test your soil's pH yourself (with a kit available at your garden center) or have it tested by a local laboratory.

Buying Healthy Plants

In mild climates, many nurseries, garden centers, and home centers stock an abundant selection of bare-root roses. For best success, choose plants that are still dormant—with buds that have not begun to swell or push into foliage.

*I*n mild-winter climates such as California, roses are frequently available as bare-root plants during the planting season at local nurseries and at large discount stores. Bare-root plants are the only kind of roses offered through mail order. Container-grown roses, however, are fast becoming the most popular form for sale at major retail nurseries and garden centers throughout North America.

Roses are usually budded, field-grown, and one to two years old when offered for sale. They are started with an understock, or base planting, of a vigorous variety such as 'Dr. Huey', *Rosa × fortuneana*, or *Rosa × odorata*. Knowing the understock is important when you're buying a rose for a specific climate. For instance, 'Dr. Huey' tolerates a wide range of conditions, from the cold winters of much of the Northeast to the hot, dry summer conditions of Southern California. If you have sandy soil and live in Florida or the Deep South, use plants budded onto *R. × fortuneana*, which are best for hot, humid conditions.

Commercial rose growers plant understock in early winter and cultivate it for six or seven months before budding the variety onto its shank just above ground level, in mid- to late spring. After one to two seasons in the field, the variety is established and ready for harvest, to be sold and planted by gardeners in winter (in mild climates) or early spring.

Bare-root roses are graded according to a uniform standard. Known as the number one grade, the top grade for large rose types (mainly hybrid tea, grandiflora, and floribunda) must have at least three strong canes $5/16$ inch in diameter, branching no higher than 3 inches above the bud union. Try to buy only the highest-quality roses; they will produce bigger bushes at little extra cost. Some growers package bare-root plants in tubes with the root system trimmed to fit the package. The same principles of grading govern these plants. In selecting packaged plants avoid wrinkled canes; they are the telltale sign of severe dehydration. Always inspect roses carefully before you buy.

Although sometimes more expensive, mail-order nurseries can supply many hard-to-find varieties, almost always offered as bare-root plants due to shipping costs. Be ready to plant them as soon as they arrive. If you must wait a few days, place in a cool spot out of the sun, and keep the roots and canes moist.

Container-grown roses, the most popular way roses are sold throughout North America, can be planted nearly anytime during the growing season. Selection is easier because you can see whether the plant is healthy and you may even see the blooms.

Soil Preparation and Planting

PREPARING SOIL FOR PLANTING

Paying careful attention to proper soil preparation and planting is your best guarantee for roses that remain lush and healthy for many years. Although it may not seem easy, you can adjust your soil to the right texture and acidity if it is not ideal. In general, a mix of equal parts of your native soil (for clay and a little sand), peat moss and compost (good humus sources), and potting soil (for more sand and humus) will closely approximate a good sandy loam. When preparing a hole for planting a rose, begin at least one week ahead and follow these steps:

DIG THE HOLE: Dig a hole 2 feet wide and 2 feet deep. Test its drainage by filling it with water. The water should drain away within several hours (if not, the soil may be too high in clay). Place one-third of the original soil back in the hole.

ADD THE AMENDMENTS: Next, fill the hole by another third with a good commercial potting soil. Finally, fill the remainder of the hole with a mixture of two parts organic compost and one part peat moss.

PREPARE THE SOIL: Thoroughly mix all ingredients and water well. Let the hole stand for about seven days, watering every two days. This waiting period allows the bacteria that fix nitrogen to build up again in the new soil.

TEST THE MIXTURE: The soil level in the hole will settle an inch or two. Before planting, test the soil with a pH meter or a paper-sensitive test kit. The soil pH should measure 5.8 to 6.8.

ADJUST THE PH: If the soil is too acidic (less than pH 5.8), add lime at the rate of $\frac{1}{3}$ cup for every 6 cubic feet of soil. If the soil is too alkaline, add $\frac{3}{4}$ teaspoon sulfur per 6 cubic feet. Floribundas need less ($\frac{1}{4}$ cup lime or $\frac{1}{2}$ teaspoon sulfur) and miniatures still less (2 tablespoons lime or $\frac{1}{4}$ teaspoon sulfur).

PREPARING BARE-ROOT ROSES FOR PLANTING

When you are ready to plant a bare-root rose, first immerse the entire bush in a bleach solution ($\frac{1}{2}$ cup household bleach per 5 gallons of water) and let it soak for 5 to 10 minutes. This sanitizes the plant, killing off any fungal spores from the growing fields. Remove the bush from the bleach solution and allow to air dry for 5 to 10 minutes.

Next, immerse the bush up to or slightly above the bud union in a vitamin B-1 solution (1 tablespoon vitamin B-1 per 5 gallons water). Vitamin B-1 is available at most home centers, garden centers, and nurseries. The bush should remain in this solution for one to three days before planting. This soaking rehydrates plants that have been out of the ground and in refrigeration for four to six weeks. B-1 is important for the new plant because of two ingredients: *thiamine hydrochloride*, an essential vitamin for growth; and *naphthalene acetic acid*, a synthetic growth regulator that speeds the development of the root system.

PLANTING BARE-ROOT ROSES

First, remove most of the soil from the prepared planting hole. Make a cone of soil in the center to accommodate the roots; spread them out evenly over the cone (if one or two roots are too long, trim them to fit the hole). Check the height of the bud union with a broom handle laid across the hole; adjust the cone of soil to keep the bud union at the correct level for your climate. As a rule, plant the bud union 2 to 3 inches below ground in climates with winter lows below -10 degrees F, and at ground level or slightly above where winter lows are -10 degrees F or warmer.

Add the remaining soil, firming it as you go, and water it with the vitamin B-1 solution to help it settle in. Mound the plant with 8 to 12 inches of mulch, and encircle it with a dam of soil to help collect water. Water it well every three or four days to get the roots off to a healthy start. When the root structure is established (in about three weeks), remove the mound of mulch a little at a time. In four to five weeks, the bud eyes should be swollen and about to burst. Watch for wrinkling on the canes—the first sign of dehydration. If this occurs, recut the canes below the wrinkling, remound the plant, and water well.

PLANTING CONTAINER-GROWN ROSES

Container-grown roses can be planted not only during bare-root season but also later through much of spring and summer. Avoid planting during very hot weather, however, or late in the day when sunlight is most intense. On the day you plant, make sure the container soil (and the soil in the planting hole) is moist but not wet.

To plant a rose that has been grown in a compressed fiber pot, follow these steps:

REMOVE THE BOTTOM: Lay the container on its side. Cut off the base of the compressed-fiber pot with a small saw. Be careful not to damage any of the roots.

PLACE IN HOLE: Place the root ball in a hole that has been dug about 2 feet wide and

PLANTING BARE-ROOT ROSES

1. Check the planting hole to make sure it's the right depth. Remove most of the soil from the hole. Make a pyramid at the bottom of the hole with the remaining soil.

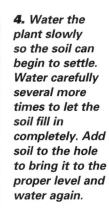

2. Test the height of the pyramid by setting the bare-root bush on it, then laying a broom handle across the top to make sure the bud union is at the correct level. Gently spread the bare roots over the cone of soil.

4. Water the plant slowly so the soil can begin to settle. Water carefully several more times to let the soil fill in completely. Add soil to the hole to bring it to the proper level and water again.

3. Carefully add the remaining soil to cover the roots, leaving a 4-inch gap at the top of the hole.

5. Mound soil or mulch over the exposed bud union or base of the plant to prevent moisture loss. Make a soil dam around the plant to collect water.

6. After a few weeks of careful watering and when the roots are established, buds and leaves will appear. It is now time to begin removing the protective mound of soil.

2 feet deep. Make certain the bud union is at the proper level (see page 14).

REMOVE THE CONTAINER: Remove the rest of the compressed-fiber pot as if you were peeling an orange. Don't worry if some roots show on the surface of the root ball.

FILL IN WITH SOIL: Fill the remaining space with a good-quality potting soil or amended soil. Press the soil gently around the root ball but avoid stamping the soil. Water, allow the soil to settle, and finish off with more potting soil. Water regularly until the roots are well-established.

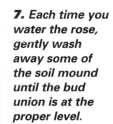

7. Each time you water the rose, gently wash away some of the soil mound until the bud union is at the proper level.

Planting and Caring for Roses in Containers

GROWING ROSES IN CONTAINERS IS EASY WHEN YOU FOLLOW THESE GUIDELINES:

■ Choose a container big enough to accommodate your plant and its potential root mass. Miniature roses are comfortable in 5- to 7-gallon pots; hybrid teas need 20- to 25-gallon containers.

■ Select your pot carefully. Plastic is light and inexpensive. If you live in a warm climate, avoid heat-absorbing black plastic pots, which may cause feeder roots near the container's sides to overheat and die. Porous containers such as terra-cotta and wood let moisture escape through the walls. This process keeps the root system cooler, but plants will need more water than plants in plastic pots. Ceramic and terra-cotta crack in cold-winter areas if kept outside during cold weather.

■ When planting, place a 2-inch layer of peat moss in the bottom of the container and around the walls. Peat moss absorbs many times its weight in water and keeps the soil mixture from drying out. Finish planting with a good potting-soil mixture and a 2- to 3-inch layer of mulch on the surface.

■ Water potted roses more frequently than in-ground roses.

Many growers keep a saucer underneath the container to catch excess moisture after watering. This technique works if you use a 2-inch peat moss layer at the bottom of the container. Without this peat moss barrier, the roots may become waterlogged and die. A dry saucer may indicate that the plant needs watering. A bonus for saucer use is that it catches excess fertilizer, which the rose can absorb later. In winter, remove the saucer from outdoor pots and allow rainfall to leach out accumulated salts, which may interfere with soil fertility. Container-grown roses need half as much fertilizer applied twice as often as in-ground plants.

Self-watering pots, which have a built-in reservoir, reduce watering chores. Shown here is 'Behold'.

For healthy roses, make sure containers have holes for drainage.

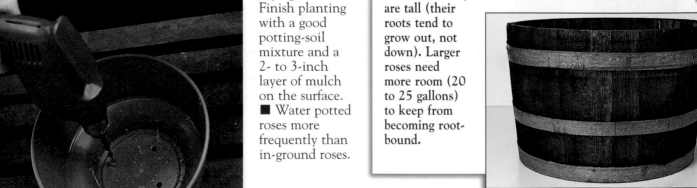

SELECTING A CONTAINER

Plastic pots are lightweight and inexpensive. Especially in hot-summer climates, choose light colors to reflect heat and help protect roots from burning. Porous terra-cotta lets moisture travel through its walls, as does wood. The evaporation keeps roots cool, but plants may need more frequent watering. There are terra-cotta-glazed containers, terra-cotta look-alikes (made of vinyl), and decorative ceramic pots. Keep in mind that ceramic and terra-cotta will crack if left outside in cold-winter areas. Large whiskey barrels make excellent containers as long as they have adequate drainage holes. All pots may become heavy when planted with roses, so equip them with casters if you can.

Miniature roses are best in containers in the 5- to 7-gallon range, wider than they are tall (their roots tend to grow out, not down). Larger roses need more room (20 to 25 gallons) to keep from becoming root-bound.

Watering and Fertilizing

Sufficient water is crucial for healthy roses. It allows vigorous growth, optimum bloom production, and strong roots. The first sign of stress from lack of water might be wilting leaves and flowers, followed by shattering flowers, shriveled flower buds, and yellowing lower leaves that eventually fall off. If the stress continues, growth slows or stops, the foliage becomes thin, few or no flowers are produced, and the plant becomes stunted. Eventually the plant will die.

Too much water can rob the soil of the oxygen needed by the roots; the resulting damage to feeder roots inhibits the ability of the plant to take up water, so the symptoms of overwatering are often similar to those of underwatering.

Roots take in water and nutrients, which travel up the stems to the leaves. In the leaves the conversion of water and nutrients into the sugars necessary to fuel growth takes place during a chemical reaction called photosynthesis. This happens when the chlorophyll in leaves is exposed to sunlight. Sugars not used immediately for growth are stored for later use; such storage is critical for healthy plants to survive stress, particularly through winter. Without adequate water, sugars cannot be produced and stored, growth becomes stunted, and the weakened plant will exhibit poor winter hardiness. Once your roses show the first signs of stress due to lack of water, such as wilting leaves, it takes ample water and five to seven days to get the plant's sugar manufacturing back to peak levels.

Large rosebushes require 2 to 5 gallons of water three times a week. In hot climates during the summer months, roses may need 3 to 5 gallons of water a day. Water roses deeply, soaking the soil to a depth of 16 to 18 inches using drip irrigation, underground sprinklers, or hand watering. Drip irrigation is efficient because it slowly releases water to the plant without runoff.

FEEDING ROSES

Well-fed roses not only reach their full size and produce abundant flowers, they also stay healthy and resist attack from insects and diseases. What you feed your roses, and how often, will depend to some extent on your soil. Roses grown in sandy soil need more frequent feeding than those grown in loam or heavier soil.

Roses need three primary nutrients—nitrogen (N), phosphorus (P), and potassium (K)—as well as a number of secondary and trace elements in order to thrive. Nitrogen promotes foliage growth; phosphorus aids healthy root and flower development; and potassium maintains vigor. Calcium, magnesium, and sulfur (secondary elements) and trace elements (boron, chlorine, copper, and iron) also promote cell and root growth.

Given proper feeding, roses will generally provide bloom cycles, or intervals between peak bloom production, about every 50 days. When the first bloom cycle has completed, initiating the second crop of roses, the fertilization needs of the rose garden change drastically. Feed once a week or at least every two weeks to maintain the health and productivity of the bush. Use a high-nitrogen, water-soluble fertilizer with an N-P-K of 8-10-8 to 20-20-20 (1 tablespoon per gallon, delivering about 2 gallons per mature bush and about 1 gallon for younger plants). Or you may broadcast about ¼ cup of granular fertilizer around your hybrid tea bushes and water it in.

In Zone 6 and colder, stop fertilizing eight weeks before the average date of the first frost to let plants harden off for their winter rest.

Whatever kind of fertilizer you use, be sure to follow exactly the directions and dosages listed on the label. Too much fertilizer can damage plants.

WATER AND FERTILIZE AT THE SAME TIME

Hose-end sprayers made to apply liquid fertilizers are handy gadgets that allow you to dispense a measured amount of water-soluble fertilizer as you water. To use a hose-end sprayer, simply add fertilizer to the reservoir as directed by the label and spray onto foliage and the soil beneath the plants. The sprayer contains a built-in proportioner that applies the correct amount of fertilizer at the correct dilution. Some allow you to attach watering wands, sprinklers, or other watering devices for added convenience. When feeding roses, be sure to use only hose-end sprayers made specifically for applying fertilizers.

A water ring is convenient for providing roses in containers with a slow, steady supply of water.

Spread granular fertilizer on moist soil above the root area, then work it in.

Fertilizer solutions can be sprayed directly onto leaves, which absorb nutrients quickly.

Pruning

Pruning gives you an annual opportunity to correct, adjust, and modify the growth of your roses to increase their flower production. Pruning times and techniques will vary somewhat with the types of roses in your garden and where you live. But in all cases it enhances the architecture of the plant, ensures a vigorous first bloom, and encourages new growth from the bud union. Removing old and damaged wood allows the plant to recuperate, and in warmer climates pruning is necessary to induce a kind of dormancy that cold-weather plants receive in winter. Even roses need a rest. During this period, plant growth is slowed and redirected toward producing those first magnificent blooms.

EQUIPMENT NEEDED

The illustration below shows how to prune a hybrid tea in a warm climate. In harsh winter climates there are far less decisions to make: Simply retain as much living tissue as possible after winter dieback.

Invest in a pair of high-quality pruning shears. You'll also need a pruning saw to remove large, woody canes at the bud union. Attempting to use pruning shears for this job usually results in damage to the bud union. For large canes a pair of lopping shears with 12- or 18-inch handles facilitates cutting without placing too much pressure on your hands. Long-handled loppers make clean, sharp cuts. Use a small wire brush about 2 inches wide and 3 inches long to help remove loose bark from the bud union. Making clean cuts and loosening bark encourages basal breaks and stimulates new growth, which cannot break through the heavy, treelike bark encountered on older bushes. Finally, buy a sturdy pair of leather gauntlet gloves or puncture-proof work gloves to protect yourself from thorns.

WHEN TO PRUNE

In general, you will be pruning just before the plant breaks dormancy after spring's final frost. This will be early in the year in warm climates and anytime between February and April in cold climates. If it's old roses you are growing, prune them after blooming. They bear flowers on last year's wood. Cut away the dead wood first—it will help you see the shape of the plant without distraction.

In cold-winter climates pruning is often reduced to one option: Simply cut back the wood that was killed in winter. Remove all diseased and dead, blackened canes, then prune a little more off each remaining cane until you see center pith that is creamy white, not brownish. Remove any weak, twiggy growth and canes that cross one another and rub in the wind.

PRUNING IN WARM CLIMATES

In warm climates, pruning can be done at any of three levels, depending on your purpose. Severe pruning (cut to leave three or four canes, 6 to 10 inches high) produces fewer but larger blooms. Moderate pruning (5 to 12 canes cut to 18 to 24 inches) makes for a larger bush. And light pruning (less than one-third of the plant is thinned out) increases the number of short-stemmed flowers that will be produced.

HYBRID TEAS AND GRANDIFLORAS:
By winter in mild climates, hybrid tea and grandifloras roses are generally 4 to 10 feet tall and looking rather lanky. Prune off one-third to one-half of the height. You can prune these canes (on an established bush) 2 to 4 feet, but in general leave four or five major canes with an average height of 3 feet. Remove the older canes; it will trigger the rose to attempt basal breaks

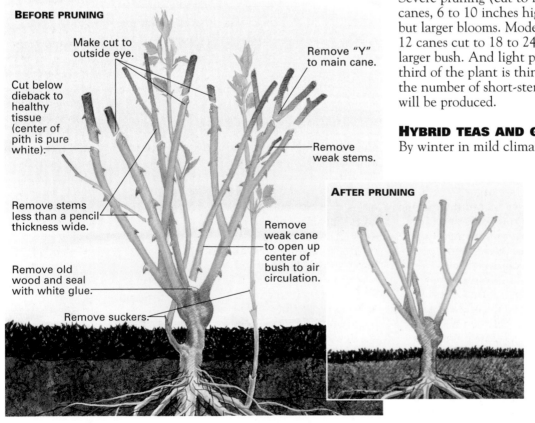

BEFORE PRUNING

Make cut to outside eye.

Cut below dieback to healthy tissue (center of pith is pure white).

Remove "Y" to main cane.

Remove weak stems.

Remove stems less than a pencil thickness wide.

Remove old wood and seal with white glue.

Remove suckers.

Remove weak cane to open up center of bush to air circulation.

AFTER PRUNING

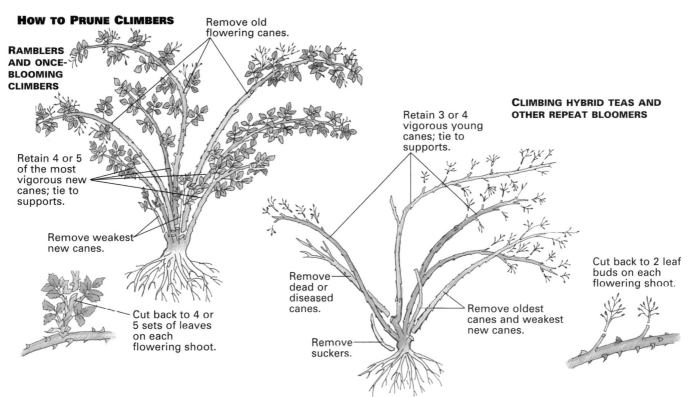

HOW TO PRUNE CLIMBERS

RAMBLERS AND ONCE-BLOOMING CLIMBERS

Remove old flowering canes.

Retain 4 or 5 of the most vigorous new canes; tie to supports.

Remove weakest new canes.

Cut back to 4 or 5 sets of leaves on each flowering shoot.

Retain 3 or 4 vigorous young canes; tie to supports.

CLIMBING HYBRID TEAS AND OTHER REPEAT BLOOMERS

Remove dead or diseased canes.

Remove suckers.

Remove oldest canes and weakest new canes.

Cut back to 2 leaf buds on each flowering shoot.

(new cane growth) in spring and is fundamental to the health of the bush.

FLORIBUNDAS AND POLYANTHAS: Cut back about one-third to one-half of the year's new growth and leave substantially more stems than you would for a hybrid tea. Leaving more canes enhances the ability of the rosebush to produce the most blooms.

MINIATURE ROSES: Most miniature roses are grown on their own roots. There is no bud union and no suckers. Precise pruning of miniature roses is very labor-intensive, and many rosarians simply use a hedge clipper to trim off the tops at a foot above the soil (height varies with the variety). Then remove any twiggy growth and open up the center of the plant to increase air circulation.

OLD GARDEN ROSES AND SHRUBS: When pruning old garden roses, avoid treating them as modern hybrid teas or floribundas. For maximum blooms, do a light grooming rather than a severe pruning. Prune only last year's growth. Prune one-time bloomers immediately after flowering; prune repeat bloomers in winter or early spring. After a few years, however, this practice makes for a very lanky bush, so each year thereafter prune back some of the oldest canes to promote basal and post-basal breaks. Keeping a proper balance between new growth and continuing old growth patterns is the secret to growing old garden roses.

CLIMBERS AND RAMBLERS: Climbers will generally not flower profusely unless the canes are trained on a horizontal plane. Cut the long-established canes to the place where

they are slightly thicker than a pencil. Then cut each side stem that has flowered to the lowest possible 5-leaflet stem, about 1 to 2 inches from the main cane. This will cause the cane to flower along its complete length.

GENERAL TIPS ON PRUNING

1. Make your pruning cuts at a 45-degree angle, about ¼ inch above a leaf axil with a dormant eye. Choose an eye on the outside of the cane and slope the cut down and away on the opposite side.

2. Always prune dead wood back to healthy tissue—green bark on the outside of the cane and white pith at the core. This is revealed after the cut is made.

3. After cutting a cane, squeeze a drop of white household glue onto it to ensure a quick recovery and provide a protective barrier against cane borers.

4. Prune the center of the bush to keep it open for maximum air circulation.

5. Remove all growth on the main canes that cannot sustain a reasonably thick stem.

6. If suckers (growth from the understock) are present, remove them as near as possible to the main root cane below the bud union.

7. Remove old woody canes by sawing them off as close to the bud union as possible.

8. After pruning, remove any remaining foliage from the canes, clean up around the bush, and discard all foliage in the trash (do not put it on the compost heap).

Prune ramblers and once-blooming climbers after they flower. Prune climbing hybrid teas and other repeat bloomers while they are dormant. Train the long canes into a horizontal position. Cut back flowering shoots, leaving four or five leaf sets. These small branches will produce next year's flowers. Canes older than four or five years should be removed to induce new growth.

Top Roses for Disease Resistance

Growing healthy, disease-free roses starts with choosing the right plants. In most climates, roses are susceptible to fungal diseases, such as rust (little orange pustules on the underside of foliage), black spot (circular black spots on leaf surfaces), and powdery mildew. Weather conditions, especially cool to moderate temperatures and humid mornings where dew is evident, promote the spread of fungal diseases. Roses in humid coastal areas are particularly vulnerable; hot, dry climates help keep fungal diseases at bay. In general, varieties with glossy, waxy foliage are less susceptible to infection because fungal spores have difficulty adhering to their smooth leaf surfaces.

Gene structure is another important factor. A rose's immune system consists of a number of phenolic compounds that prevent infection. Lack of moisture or nutrients can cause a drop in these protective chemicals, permitting infections to take hold. Fortunately some plants have a fairly high resistance to fungal diseases—even in cool, damp weather.

The varieties recommended in this section are highly resistant to fungal infections.

New Zealand ('MACgenev')

■ *Hybrid tea, light pink, 1989, McGredy*

Soft creamy-pink blooms (30 to 35 petals) of perfect symmetry exude delicious honeysuckle fragrance. Largest bloom size occurs in cool climates. Foliage is lush, glossy dark-green and completely disease-free. Plant grows 4 to 6 feet tall, profusely covered with blooms all growing season. Zones 5 through 10.

Gizmo ('WEKcatlard')

■ *Miniature, orange blend, 1998, Carruth*

Single-petaled scarlet-red flowers with a white eye completely cover this plant all summer. The blooms are long-lasting, and resist fading even in hot sun. Plants are small (14 to 20 inches tall), healthy, and vigorous, with excellent glossy green foliage. Mild apple scent. Zones 5 through 10.

Knock Out ('RADrazz')

■ *Shrub, red blend, 1999, Radler, AARS*

The epitome of the new generation of roses, this high performer has demonstrated nearly complete resistance to black spot and excellent resistance to other fungal diseases. Reportedly its healthy-looking glossy blue-green foliage is distasteful to Japanese beetles too. The bush is literally covered all summer long with an explosion of brilliant, single-petaled raspberry-red flowers that have a very light fragrance and last a long time. In cool climates, color becomes more intense. Plants are 4 to 6 feet tall. Zones 4 through 10.

'The Fairy'

■ *Polyantha, light pink, 1932, Bentall*

This award winner is the standard for low-maintenance, disease-resistant shrub roses used in landscaping projects. Seemingly never out of bloom, it has huge clusters of small, ruffled, soft pink flowers all summer. Its cool pale-pink color makes it ideal in the mixed border, especially if pruned as a low-growing shrub. Little fragrance. Plant grows 3 to 4 feet tall. Zones 4 through 10.

Carefree Sunshine ('RADsun')

■ *Shrub, medium yellow, 2002, Radler*

This sister variety to Knock Out bears lightly fragrant, brilliant yellow flowers in abundance all summer. It exhibits terrific resistance to black spot even though yellow roses are prone to this fungus. Its growth habit is somewhat more upright than Knock Out, with glossy green foliage all the way to the ground. Zones 4 through 10.

MORE EASY ROSES WITH EXCELLENT DISEASE RESISTANCE

Blueberry Hill ('WEKcryplag')

■ *Floribunda, mauve, 1999, Carruth*

Small clusters of lilac blooms (12 to 25 petals). Leathery dark green foliage. 3 to 4 feet. Zones 5–10. (Photo page 79.)

Gemini ('JACnepal')

■ *Hybrid tea, pink blend, 1999, Zary, AARS*

Vigorous plant with opulent supply of symmetrical pink blooms (35 to 40 petals) on long stems. 5 to 6 feet. Zones 5–10. (Photo page 7.)

Gourmet Popcorn ('WEOpop')

■ *Miniature, white, 1986, Desamero*

A highly rated ground cover when planted 2 feet apart. Abundant large clusters of white blooms. 2 to 3 feet. Zones 4–10. (Photos pages 9, 34.)

Iceberg ('KORbin')

■ *Floribunda, white, 1958, Kordes, WFRS*

Voted World's Favorite Rose in 1983. Massive displays of attractive pure white flowers (20 to 25 petals). 3 to 4 feet. Zones 5–10. (Photos pages 9, 32.)

Ingrid Bergman ('POUlman')

■ *Hybrid tea, dark red, 1984, Olesen, WFRS*

Large blooms on long straight stems. Voted World's Favorite Rose in 2000. 5 to 6 feet. Zones 5–10. (Photo page 68.)

'Loving Touch'

■ *Miniature, apricot blend, 1983, Jolly, AOE*

Well-rounded bush with an abundance of exhibition-quality flowers. 12 to 18 inches. Zones 5–10. (Photo page 67.)

Moonstone ('WEKcryland')

■ *Hybrid tea, white, 1998, Carruth*

Ivory-white flowers (40 petals, 4 inches wide, slight fragrance) with delicate pink edging, borne singly on a tall bush covered with tough, heat-tolerant green foliage. 5 to 7 feet. Zones 5–10. (Photo page 31.)

Napa Valley ('POUlino')

■ *Shrub, medium red, 1995, Olesen*

An excellent ground cover with bright crimson blooms on a compact plant about 2 feet in diameter, 12 to 20 inches tall. Zones 4–9.

Pillow Fight ('WEKpipogop')

■ *Shrub, white, 1999, Carruth*

First variety in new generation of shrublets that displays flowers all summer. Massive sprays contain as many as 50 blooms. 2 to 3 feet. Zones 4–9. (Photos pages 9, 66.)

'Playboy'

■ *Floribunda, red blend, 1976, Cocker*

Popular single-petaled variety. Rich blend of orange and scarlet flowers with a bright yellow eye. 4 to 5 feet. Zones 5–9. (Photo page 32.)

'Sea Foam'

■ *Shrub, white, 1964, Schwartz*

Double florets have delicate fragrance and can sustain bad weather. Ideal for weeping standard. 2 to 8 feet. Zones 5–10.

Showbiz ('TANweieke')

■ *Floribunda, medium red, 1983, Tantau, AARS*

Massive sprays of long-lasting brilliant scarlet red blooms (20 to 25 petals) on strong, straight stems. 3 to 4 feet. Zones 5–10. (Photo page 6.)

Top Roses for Cold Climates

*I*f you live in a cold-winter climate (Zones 3 through 5), one option you have is to plant nonhardy roses, then take extensive measures to protect them from loss during cold weather. However, a better solution is to choose varieties likely to survive severe winters in your area.

For many years, the only roses not requiring winter protection were the native wild roses of North America: *R. acicularis* (Arctic rose), *R. arkansana* (Arkansas rose), *R. blanda* (Hudson's Bay rose), *R. carolina* (Carolina or pasture rose), *R. virginiana* (Virginia rose), *R. woodsii* (mountain rose), and *R. setigera* (prairie rose). Some old garden roses and a few double-flowered hybrids of *R. rugosa* were also hardy. Unfortunately most of these winter-hardy varieties are sprawling bushes with single-petaled blooms that only appear for a single brief season in early summer.

Today a much broader selection of hardy roses is available. Breeders such as Griffith Buck of Iowa and organizations such as the Research Branch of Agriculture Canada have bred winter-hardy repeat-blooming roses—in the Canadian Explorer and Parkland series—that are double- to full-petaled. The roses on these two pages require no winter protection and provide color throughout the summer.

Carefree Beauty ('BUCbi')
■ *Shrub, medium pink, 1977, Buck*
This popular repeat bloomer bred by Griffith Buck produces small sprays of up to 4 florets each that open to reveal large (4 inches wide, 10 to 20 petals), fragrant flowers of a rich pink color. Foliage is smooth and olive green and rarely shows signs of disease. Plant is upright (4 to 5 feet tall) and nearly always covered in flowers. It can be grown to form a neat hedge. Attractive orange-red hips last from fall through winter. Zones 4 through 10.

Marie-Victorin ('AC Marie Victorin')
■ *Hybrid kordesii, pink blend, 1999, Agriculture Canada*
Small clusters of 3-inch blossoms (20 to 30 petals) on this hardy, disease-resistant plant are an unusual blend of peach-pink and yellow. They have a slight fragrance. The semiglossy foliage is medium green on an upright, arched plant 3 to 4 feet tall. From the Canadian Explorer series. Zones 3 through 10.

'William Baffin'
■ *Hybrid kordesii, deep pink, 1983, Svedja*
Semidouble blooms are strawberry pink with a touch of white toward the brilliant yellow stamens at the center. Florets grow in clusters with up to 30 blooms per stem from summer to autumn. The flowers have little or no fragrance. The upright plant (10 to 12 feet tall) makes this rose usable as an impenetrable hedge or a climber over a fence or wall. Its slightly arching stems are covered with glossy, disease-resistant foliage. One of the Canadian Explorer series, named after the famous explorer who sought the Northwest Passage. Zones 2 through 9.

'Morden Blush'

■ *Shrub, light pink, 1988, Agriculture Canada*
This shrub rose bears light pink flowers that
fade to a warm ivory. Smallish double blooms
have about 50 petals and last for weeks.
Florets generally come in sprays of 2 to 5
blooms. Foliage is medium green with a matte
finish. The plant is low-growing, 2 to 5 feet
tall. This is one of the many hardy roses
developed as Parkland Roses at the Morden
Research Center in Manitoba, Canada. Zones
2 through 10.

'Prairie Flower'

■ *Shrub, red blend, 1975, Buck*
Single-petaled cardinal red flowers (7 petals,
2 to 3 inches wide) with an attractive white
eye appear in small clusters and emit a light,
old-rose fragrance. Erect bushes reach 5 to 6
feet tall, with leathery, dark green foliage.
Bred to withstand harsh winters, it needs
little or no protection. Zones 3 through 9.

MORE EASY ROSES FOR COLD CLIMATES

'Distant Drums'
■ *Shrub, mauve, 1985, Buck*
Large rose-purple blossoms in sprays of 2 to 10
florets. Myrrh fragrance; leathery foliage; vigorous,
erect bush. 5 to 6 feet. Zones 4–9.

'Golden Unicorn'
■ *Shrub, yellow blend, 1985, Buck*
Large cupped double flowers (28 petals, slight
fragrance) in clusters. Yellow with orange-red
edges. Foliage is dark olive-green and leathery.
4 to 5 feet. Zones 4–9.

'Hansa'
■ *Hybrid rugosa, medium red, 1905, Schaum &
Van Tol*
A classic hardy rose with wrinkled, dark green
foliage and large double red blooms (3 inches
wide). Clove-rose fragrance. 4 to 5 feet. Zones 3–9.

'Henry Kelsey'
■ *Hybrid kordesii, medium red, 1984, Svedja*
Prolific small clusters of semidouble bright red
flowers with yellow stamens. Spicy fragrance.
Useful as a climber with little winter protection.
6 to 8 feet. Zones 3–9. (Photo page 65.)

'John Cabot'
■ *Hybrid kordesii, medium red, 1978, Svedja*
Semidouble bright red flowers. Two main flushes of
bloom are normal, but repeats much better if grown
in full sun and fertilized. 6 to 10 feet. Zones 3–10.
(Photo page 39.)

'Martin Frobisher'
■ *Hybrid rugosa, light pink, 1968, Svedja*
Very hardy, vigorous, upright rose with blush pink
blooms (semidouble). Slightly fragrant. Bush habit
is very open and sparse. 5 to 6 feet. Zones 2–11.

'Morden Amorette'
■ *Shrub, deep pink, 1977, Marshall*
Large double flowers (28 petals) on medium-sized
bush. Slight fragrance. Glossy dark green foliage.
2 to 3 feet. Zones 3–10.

'Prairie Harvest'
■ *Shrub, light yellow, 1985, Buck*
Large blossoms (4 inches wide) with 40+ petals,
singly or in sprays of up to 15 florets. Moderate
fragrance, leathery foliage, upright plant. 4 to 5
feet. Zones 4–9.

'Stanwell Perpetual'
■ *Hybrid spinosissima, white, 1838, Lee*
Quartered soft apricot to blush pink to creamy
white flowers with strong fragrance. Thorny
bushes good for hedges or screening. 3 to 5 feet.
Zones 3–9. (Photo page 37.)

'Therese Bugnet'
■ *Hybrid rugosa, medium pink, 1950, Bugnet*
Large, old-fashioned, ruffled double blooms of lilac
pink with a soft fragrance. Excellent choice for the
coldest climates. 5 to 6 feet. Zones 2–9.

Top Roses for Hot Climates

Many varieties of roses are suited to subtropical, tropical, or desert areas. To thrive in these conditions, the foliage must be robust and thick, and the blooms must withstand temperatures exceeding 90 degrees F.

In subtropical and tropical climates, the high humidity that accompanies high heat can set up the conditions for an epidemic of black spot. The varieties listed here have the necessary characteristics to survive hot climates—humid or dry—as well as resist black spot.

Brandy ('AROcad')

■ *Hybrid tea, apricot blend, 1981, Swim & Christensen, AARS*
Elegant pointed buds on long straight stems begin a vivid deep apricot that fades slightly to a rich warm apricot upon opening. In warm climate zones the flowers can become huge, almost the size of saucers. Fully open blooms perch atop stems densely covered with large glossy leaves. Fragrance is mild tea. Plants grow 5 to 6 feet tall and generally perform best in their second year. Most need winter protection in severe cold-winter climates. Zones 6 through 10.

Crystalline ('ARObipy')

■ *Hybrid tea, white, 1987, Christensen and Carruth*
Originally bred for the cut flower trade, this immaculate white hybrid tea boasts symmetrical blooms (35 petals, 3 to 4 inches wide) with a spicy or sweet tea fragrance. It is popular throughout the United States as a garden rose; its breeding as a florist rose makes it especially suited to hot climates.

Plants grow 5 to 6 feet tall. Foliage is semiglossy, medium green with a distinctive wrinkled pattern. Zones 5 through 10.

Sunset Celebration ('FRYxotic')

■ *Hybrid tea, apricot blend, 1999, Fryer, AARS*
This prize-winning variety from England produces flowers (40 petals, 4 to 5 inches across, fruity fragrance) of creamy apricot-amber, usually one bloom per stem, that hold their color well without fading, even in hot climates. Leaves are large and medium green. The plant habit is upright and well-rounded, reaching 5 to 6 feet by the end of the growing season. Zones 5 through 10.

MORE EASY ROSES FOR HOT CLIMATES

French Lace ('JAClace')
■ *Floribunda, white, 1980, Warriner, AARS*
The epitome of pastel roses. Symmetrical flowers (30 petals, 3 to 4 inches wide, mild fruity fragrance) are pearly white verging on pastel apricot. 3 to 4 feet. Zones 6–10. (Photos pages 33, 69.)

Intrigue ('JACum')
■ *Floribunda, mauve, 1982, Warriner, AARS*
Popular in warm climates because of heat tolerance. Buds are deep purple-red, opening to velvety-plum flowers (30 petals) with a strong citrus perfume. Dark green foliage on a medium-sized plant. 3 to 4 feet. Zones 5–10. (Photo page 7.)

'Mister Lincoln'
■ *Hybrid tea, dark red, 1964, Swim & Weeks, AARS*
The landmark in red roses. Flowers a velvety red (35 petals, 3 to 4 inches wide). Powerful damask perfume. 5 to 6 feet. Zones 5–10. (Photos pages 6, 10.)

Moonstone ('WEKcryland')
■ *Hybrid tea, white, 1998, Carruth*
Flowers (40 petals, 4 inches wide, slight fragrance) are ivory with a delicate pink edging. Borne singly on tall bush covered with tough, heat-tolerant, medium green foliage. Plant becomes a massive, tall structure by the end of the season. 5 to 7 feet. Zones 5–10. (Photo page 31.)

'Oklahoma'
■ *Hybrid tea, dark red, 1964, Swim & Weeks*
All-time classic with dark red blooms (48 petals, 4 to 5 inches wide, intense fragrance) on strong stems with attractive matte, dark green foliage. 5 to 6 feet. Zones 5–10.

'Royal Highness'
■ *Hybrid tea, light pink, 1962, Swim & Weeks, AARS*
Known as the sovereign of elegance and style. Opulent flowers (40 petals, 5 to 6 inches wide, sweet tea scent) of pale porcelain pink. Foliage is a lustrous, bright medium green. 5 to 7 feet. Zones 5–10. (Photo page 77.)

Showbiz ('TANweieke')
■ *Floribunda, medium red, 1983, Tantau, AARS*
German variety with fire engine red blooms in gigantic clusters (as many as 30 flowers on one stem). Foliage a glossy green and disease-resistant. 3 to 4 feet. Zones 5–10. (Photo page 6.)

St. Patrick ('WEKamanda')
■ *Hybrid tea, medium yellow, 1999, Strickland, AARS*
Unusual green buds open slowly to golden-yellow blooms with greenish outer petals. 4 to 5 feet. Zones 5–10. (Photos pages 8, 31.)

'Uncle Joe'
■ *Hybrid tea, dark red, 1972, Kern Rose Nursery*
Extremely large, full blooms (80+ petals, 4 to 5 inches wide) require high heat and humidity for best show. Large, vigorous plants with leathery, dark green leaves. 6 to 8 feet. Zones 5–10.

Sun Flare ('JACjam')
■ *Floribunda, medium yellow, 1981, Warriner, AARS*
Among floribundas this is a classic variety because of its abundant clusters of brilliant yellow blooms (30 petals, 3 inches wide, 3 to 13 florets per stem) on very straight strong stems. Plants are vigorous and low-growing, reaching 3 to 4 feet tall, with small glossy deep green leaves. Zones 5 through 10.

Bonica ('MEIdomonac')
■ *Shrub, medium pink, 1985, Meilland, AARS*
This easy-to-grow shrub set the standard for a whole new generation of landscape shrubs. Small clusters of double clear pink flowers (40+ petals) cover it all growing season. Low-growing and rounded (about 3 to 4 feet tall) with lush, healthy green foliage, it is well-suited for massing and hedges. Zones 4 through 10.

Top Roses for Partial Shade

To grow most roses successfully, all-day sunshine is a must. Yet even if your garden receives sun for only four hours a day, one group of roses assures results. These roses can open fully in diminished sunlight and resist the fungal diseases that shady sites promote. Many belong to a petal group known as singles (5 to 12 petals) or doubles (12 to 20 petals) with glossy leaves that resist mildew and black spot. Plants with shiny leaves can thwart infection because their wax coating forms a natural shield that disease spores can't stick to. These roses need sufficient heat for the petals to open naturally.

Although most blooms with more than 40 petals may never open properly in low-light conditions, there are a few exceptions. For those who wish to grow full-petaled roses in shady conditions, several varieties are recommended here.

Amber Queen ('HARroony')
■ *Floribunda, apricot blend, 1983, Harkness, AARS*
Golden-apricot flowers of this English import (30 petals, 2 to 3 inches wide, sweet and spicy scent) rarely fade, even in strong sun. Blooms repeat every five weeks. Its medium green foliage resists most diseases, even in partial shade. An ideal border plant, about 2 to 3 feet tall. Zones 5 through 10.

English Garden ('AUSbuff')
■ *Shrub, apricot blend, 1990, Austin*
This modern shrub from David Austin's English Rose series bears large, fully double cupped flowers (40 petals, 4 inches wide) of apricot-yellow with a wonderful old-fashioned form and fragrance. The plant is 4 to 5 feet tall, upright, and easily grown in a large tub. It will need pruning to keep it from growing too tall in warm climates. Zones 4 through 9.

The Prince ('AUSvelvet')
■ *Shrub, dark red, 1993, Austin*
Rich deep crimson to royal purple petals intricately fold against their neighbors to form a shallow rosette (100 petals, 4 inches wide). Old garden rose fragrance. Even in warm climates, the plant does not get much above 2 to 3 feet tall. Its deep red roses look stunning in dappled shade, where its foliage remains healthy and disease-free. Zones 4 through 9.

MORE EASY ROSES FOR PART SHADE

Abraham Darby ('AUScot')
■ *Shrub, orange pink, 1990, Austin*
Old-fashioned large-cupped very fragrant blooms in rich shades of apricot at times touched with gold. 4 to 6 feet. Zones 4–9. (Photo page 39.)

'Angel Face'
■ *Floribunda, mauve, 1968, Swim & Weeks, AARS*
Ruffled blooms (25 to 30 petals) with a strong aroma of sweet citrus appear continuously all season. Small plants grow 2 to 3 feet tall and wide. Zones 5–9.

'Blush Noisette'
■ *Noisette, white, before 1817*
Nearly thornless bush with delicate soft pink flowers (30 petals) in clusters of 6 to 12 florets. Lush, dark foliage. 6 to 7 feet. Zones 7–10.

'Buff Beauty'
■ *Hybrid musk, apricot blend, 1939, Bentall*
Apricot yellow flowers (30 petals, 4 inches wide, moderate tea fragrance) in clusters of 12 florets on relatively smooth arching canes. Dark green foliage. 4 to 5 feet. Zones 5–9.

Golden Celebration ('AUSgold')
■ *Shrub, deep yellow, 1993, Austin*
Rich deep golden yellow flowers (5 inches wide) have an old garden rose appearance, cupped and containing as many as 70 to 80 petals. Excellent old-rose fragrance. 5 to 8 feet. Zones 4–10. (Photo page 81.)

'Gruss an Aachen'
■ *Floribunda, light pink, 1909, Geduldig*
Orange-red and yellow buds open to flesh pink blooms that fade to creamy white (40 petals, 3 to 4 inches wide, sweet fragrance). A small plant with rich foliage and nodding stems. 3 to 4 feet. Zones 5–9.

'Mlle Cecile Brunner, Climbing'
■ *Climbing polyantha, light pink, 1894, Ducher*
A beloved old-timer with large, airy clusters of small, pointed, eggshell white buds opening to creamy pale pink blooms. Canes can scramble over a garden shed or pergola. 10 to 20 feet. Zones 6–9.

'New Dawn'
■ *Climber, light pink, 1930, Van Fleet, WFRS*
Pale cameo pink flowers (35 petals, 3 inches wide, sweet rose scent) in massive quantities throughout the year on canes that often reach 12 to 20 feet. Zones 4–10. (Photo page 63.)

'Playboy'
■ *Floribunda, red blend, 1976, Cocker*
Popular variety with single-petaled flowers in a rich blend of orange and scarlet with a bright yellow eye. 4 to 5 feet. Zones 5–9. (Photo page 32.)

'Sally Holmes'
■ *Shrub, white, 1976, Holmes*
Flowers in large clusters like a hydrangea (5 to 8 petals, 4 inches wide, slight fragrance), creamy white to pink in bud and pure white on opening. Needs plenty of space. Much better against a wall than in a bed. 6 to 12 feet. Zones 4–10. (Photos pages 6, 39.)

'Ballerina'
■ *Hybrid musk, medium pink, 1937, Bentall*
A profusely blooming rose with large clusters of medium pink flowers and a white eye. The first summer flush of flowers is so dense it often obscures the abundant green foliage. After a short pause the second flush nearly equals the first. Plant is a graceful, well-rounded bush, 3 feet tall. Zones 4 through 10.

'Cornelia'
■ *Hybrid musk, pink blend, 1925, Pemberton*
Double rosette-shaped flowers in large arching trusses range from strawberry-flushed yellow to pale apricot-copper to salmon-pink with an orange base. Fragrance is a powerful sweet musk. Vigorous plants can provide sufficient cane length (6 to 8 feet) to cascade over a wall or be trained as a pillar. Canes are thornless; the glossy foliage is dark green tinged with bronze. Zones 4 through 10.

Ortho's All-Stars

Roses arouse strong passions. Some folks like their beauty, some their fragrance. There are so many characteristics from which to choose that choosing the best of thousands in a traditional rose class can be difficult. This section makes selecting great roses easy because we do the work. Each all-star variety must fulfill five main requirements (see Selection Standards, below) to make the honor roll. So if you're looking for the best rose by class instead of a rose for a particular landscape use, Ortho's All-Stars are for you.

Diana, Princess of Wales is a new hybrid introduced in 1998 by Jackson & Perkins in honor of a great humanitarian. Its description as an Ortho All-Star Hybrid Tea is on page 31.

SELECTION STANDARDS

■ **CLIMATE-HARDY:** The variety must withstand severe winters and/or heat.

■ **VIGOROUS GROWTH HABIT:** Overall plant growth and shape must be vigorous, pleasing, and unaffected by temperature extremes.

■ **DISEASE-RESISTANT:** Plants must be resistant to black spot, powdery mildew, and rust within a wide range of climates.

■ **FRAGRANT:** Variety should have a light to sweet fragrance in all climates.

■ **LOW-MAINTENANCE:** Plants must need only minimum attention (such as deadheading) during the growing season.

ROSE AWARDS

ALL-AMERICA ROSE SELECTIONS (AARS)
The All-America Rose Selections (AARS) is a nonprofit organization of U.S. rose producers and introducers. It tests new rose varieties and recommends the best to the general public. Only a few outstanding varieties bear the title "AARS Winner" each year. This award is a hallmark of excellence, indicating that the variety can be grown in almost any climate. The testing protocol is rigorous.

Varieties are evaluated for two years in two dozen specially designated AARS gardens throughout the United States that offer varying levels of heat, drought, cold winds, insects, and diseases. They must survive the harsh winters of Illinois, the subtropical climate of Florida, and the Mediterranean climate of California. Not all varieties chosen for this honor are exhibition roses. In many cases judges select good garden varieties for their abundant flowers or their speed of bloom cycle. Since this program began in 1940, nearly 200 varieties have received the award.

AWARD OF EXCELLENCE FOR MINIATURE ROSES (AOE)
Each year the American Rose Society (ARS) tests miniature roses. Entries are tested for two years. The ARS wants to foster the development of new and better roses in the United States, to establish gardens for testing new varieties, to acquaint people with

MODERN ROSE-BREEDING TRENDS

During the last half of the 20th century, breeders focused on producing elegant hybrid teas and floribundas in every color imaginable. Rose buyers supported these new varieties, and hybrid teas soon cornered the rose business. Though breeders succeeded in creating stunning summer-long blooms, they often abandoned desirable traits such as vigor, disease resistance, and fragrance. This mania for form also preoccupied miniature-rose breeders, who produced small versions of hybrid teas.

The rekindled interest in old roses and the introduction of modern shrub roses broke the fixation on color and hybrid tea form. By altering selection criteria and broadening bloodlines, growers developed repeat-blooming plants with lavish old-fashioned blooms, delightful fragrance, modern colors (such as yellow, salmon, and scarlet), and attractive, shrubby shapes. The rose-buying public embraced this evolutionary step. Today, breeders are introducing a host of modern shrubs that incorporate hardiness, perfume, vigor, and disease resistance. Other types of roses, such as ground covers and hybrid teas, have also benefited from these advances and merit places on Ortho's all-star list.

Santa Claus is a miniature introduced by Poulsen in 1991 that provides a stunning display when massed as an edging or in low beds. Its description as an Ortho All-Star Miniature is on page 35.

worthy roses, to award superior new roses, and to publicize and recommend those award-winning varieties. The test gardens for miniatures are at the American Rose Society in Shreveport, Louisiana, and at six other locations throughout the country. Almost 70 miniature roses have received this award since the start of the program in 1975.

ARS MINIATURE ROSE HALL OF FAME

Established in 1999 by the American Rose Society, this award program recognizes sustained achievement by a popular variety existing in commerce for more than 20 years. To date there have been 10 recipients.

WORLD FEDERATION OF ROSE SOCIETIES (WFRS) ROSE HALL OF FAME

Every three years the World Federation of Rose Societies chooses one rose to receive this title. To date 10 varieties have been honored.

INTERNATIONAL ROSE TRIALS

Throughout the world many rose trials award prizes to winning varieties. Trials usually display test varieties in a public park to illustrate the value of modern roses as free-blooming, leafy, healthy, and beautiful flowering plants. Breeders, professionals, and amateurs submit varieties for testing. The most recent garden to establish an International Rose Trials Grounds is Rose Hills Memorial Park in Whittier, California.

Ortho's All-Star Hybrid Teas and Grandifloras

shaped flowers on long stems. Although the first hybrid tea was introduced in 1867, it wasn't until 1945 and the introduction of 'Peace' that hybridizing hybrid teas took off. There are now more than 10,000 hybrid teas in every imaginable color except true blue or black.

Breeders introduced the first grandiflora, an outgrowth of hybrid teas, in 1954. Grandifloras display the characteristics of a hybrid tea and also bear clusters, or trusses, of flowers. They grow to a commanding height of 6 to 8 feet tall.

Barbra Streisand ('WEKquaneze')
■ *Hybrid tea, mauve, 1999, Carruth*
This most recent example of using rose breeding techniques is a hybrid tea with all the desirable qualities of an Ortho all-star. The lavender blooms (sweet rose fragrance) are blushed with purple, the depth of the blush deepening in cool climates. The flowers are set off by glossy deep green foliage that is remarkably disease-resistant. Plants grow 3 to 6 feet tall. Zones 5 through 10.

Veteran's Honor ('JACopper') ✓
■ *Hybrid tea, dark red, 1999, Zary*
Sculptured 2-inch buds on this impeccable red rose spiral into grandiose floral masterpieces (25 to 30 petals). The deep red color holds well without fading even through the hottest sunny days. Flowers can survive for weeks in the garden, are excellent for cutting, and withstand rain showers without blemishing. The plant is extremely vigorous and upright, 5 to 7 feet tall. Zones 5 through 10.

Hybrid teas are repeat bloomers that create a striking display when massed in rose beds and borders. Because of their high-centered, sculptural blooms that are long-lasting when cut, they are popular exhibition flowers in rose shows. Plants have an upright habit and reach 5 to 6 feet high and an average width of 3 to 4 feet by the end of the growing season. They typically produce one flower at the end of each long stem at regular intervals of 35 to 45 days. Spent flowers must be removed to induce the next flowering cycle. Deadheading is best done by cutting the stem to the nearest 5-leaflet set of foliage with a stem thickness greater than a pencil. Occasionally hybrid teas form clusters of flowers at the end of stems. Removing the side buds of the cluster encourages larger, more perfectly shaped single blooms on longer stems for cutting or exhibition.

Today the hybrid tea has become the most popular class of modern roses, easily recognizable by large symmetrically

St. Patrick ('WEKamanda') ✓
■ *Hybrid tea, medium yellow, 1999, Strickland, AARS*
Novel chartreuse-shaded buds spiral open to reveal cool-yellow flowers of remarkable endurance. This slow-opening rose (30 to 35 petals) is ideal for warm, humid climates, in which the outer edges of the petals shade to green. In cool climates the blooms show a touch of gold. Fragrance is minimal. Foliage is a lovely matte dark green that rarely shows signs of disease. This well-rounded bush reaches 4 to 5 feet tall. Zones 5 through 10.

MORE ORTHO ALL-STAR HYBRID TEAS AND GRANDIFLORAS

Gemini ('JACnepal')
■ *Hybrid tea, pink blend, 1999, Zary, AARS*
Exceptionally vigorous with an abundance of pure pink flowers (35 to 40 petals). 5 to 6 feet. Zones 5–10. (Photo page 7.)

Ingrid Bergman ('POUlman') ✓
■ *Hybrid tea, dark red, 1984, Olesen, WFRS*
Blooms (35 to 40 petals) supported on long stems covered with glossy deep green foliage. Voted World's Favorite Rose in 2000. 5 to 6 feet. Zones 5–10. (Photo page 68.)

Kardinal ('KORlingo') ✓
■ *Hybrid tea, medium red, 1986, Kordes*
Blooms (30 to 35 petals) are perfectly formed but can be small in hot climates. 4 to 6 feet. Zones 5–10. (Photo page 76.)

New Zealand ('MACgenev')
■ *Hybrid tea, light pink, 1989, McGredy*
Creamy pink blooms on long stems. Lush fragrance. 4 to 6 feet. Zones 5–10. (Photo page 20.)

Olympiad ('MACauck')
■ *Hybrid tea, medium red, 1982, McGredy, AARS*
A fine red hybrid tea (30 to 35 petals) in the classical tradition of the 20th century. 4 to 6 feet. Zones 5–10. (Photo page 7.)

Perfect Moment ('KORwilma')
■ *Hybrid tea, red blend, 1989, Kordes, AARS*
Dazzling red blooms (25 to 30 petals) with an electric yellow inner glow. 4 to 7 feet. Zones 5–10. (Photo page 6.)

'Queen Elizabeth' ✓
■ *Grandiflora, medium pink, 1954, Lammerts, AARS*
A legendary grandiflora (about 35 petals) that adorns gardens all over the world. 6 to 10 feet. Zones 5–10. (Photo page 7.)

Sunset Celebration ('FRYxotic')
■ *Hybrid tea, apricot blend, 1999, Fryer, AARS, WFRS*
Exceptional in all climates. Blooms (35 to 40 petals) are rich warm peach. 4 to 6 feet. Zones 5–10. (Photo page 24.)

Timeless ('JACecond')
■ *Hybrid tea, medium pink, 1998, Zary, AARS*
Long shapely buds spiral open slowly to lustrous evenly pink blooms (about 25 petals). 4 to 6 feet. Zones 5–10.

'Uncle Joe'
■ *Hybrid tea, dark red, 1972, Kern Rose Nursery*
A favorite hybrid tea for warm, humid southern climates. Large perfectly formed blooms (50+ petals). 4 to 8 feet. Zones 5–10.

Moonstone ('WEKcryland') ✓
■ *Hybrid tea, white, 1998, Carruth*
This rose seems to thrive on indifference. The perfectly symmetrical blooms, edged with delicate pink, have a fragrance reminiscent of mild tea and rose. The stems are long and straight, perfect for cutting, and the lush large leaves seem impervious to disease. The plant is vigorous and large, growing 5 to 7 feet tall and producing abundant blooms every five weeks. Zones 5 through 10.

Diana, Princess of Wales ('JACshaq') ✓
■ *Hybrid tea, pink blend, 1998, Zary*
Classified as a hybrid tea, this vigorous, well-rounded bush reaches a height of 4 to 6 feet and has an alluring effect when planted in mass. It has a strong tendency to produce small clusters rather than set one bloom atop each stem. Ivory petals (30 to 35 per flower) are overlaid with a clear pink blush. The 4- to 5-inch flowers have a sweet fragrance. Zones 5 through 10.

Ortho's All-Star Floribundas and Polyanthas

Floribundas provide massive, colorful, long-lasting garden displays. They make attractive, low-growing hedges and excellent border accents. Second only to hybrid teas and grandifloras in popularity, floribundas grow 3 to 5 feet tall and bear profuse numbers of flowers in clusters, or trusses. More than one bloom in each truss is open at any given time. The distinct advantage of floribundas is their ability to bloom continually, whereas hybrid teas bloom in cycles of six to seven weeks. Floribundas often are hardier, easier to care for, and more reliable in wet weather than hybrid teas. Floribundas also offer a wider range of flower forms—single-petaled, semidouble, double, and rosette.

Polyanthas are sturdy plants that are smaller than floribundas. They produce large clusters of 1-inch flowers and have small leaves. Polyanthas and floribundas descend from *R. multiflora*, a wild rose with an abundance of little flowers. Breeders improved it for garden display because it had the advantage of producing clusters of flowers on one stem rather than a solitary bloom.

Livin' Easy ('HARwelcome')
■ *Floribunda, orange blend, 1992, Harkness, AARS*

This is a consistent top performer in all climates. Showy clusters of frilly apricot-orange flowers (25 to 30 petals) cover the bush nonstop all summer. Its glossy foliage is highly resistant to disease and apparently impervious to black spot. Plants require little deadheading or pruning during the growing season. Vigorous bushes grow 3 to 4 feet tall. Zones 5 through 10.

'Playboy'
■ *Floribunda, red blend, 1976, Cocker*

This Scottish import combines the simplicity of a single-petaled rose with rambunctious colors—orange and scarlet with a yellow eye. Medium-sized clusters of large flowers (smaller in hot climates) on strong, straight stems emit a sweet apple fragrance. Glossy green foliage is extremely disease-resistant. Easy and trouble-free. Grows 4 to 5 feet tall. Zones 5 through 9.

Iceberg ('KORbin')
■ *Floribunda, white, 1958, Kordes, WFRS*

Voted the world's most popular rose in 1983, this variety is grown as a standard, climber, or handsome, rounded bush. Throughout the growing season, its attractive, pure white flowers (20 to 25 petals) appear in open, airy sprays at the ends of long stems. Foliage is lush, glossy, and always healthy. In cool climates blooms can display an occasional flush of pink. Plant grows 3 to 4 feet tall. Zones 5 through 10.

MORE ORTHO ALL-STAR FLORIBUNDAS AND POLYANTHAS

'Angel Face'
■ *Floribunda, mauve, 1968, Swim & Weeks, AARS*
Ruffled blooms (25 to 30 petals) with a strong aroma of sweet citrus. 2 to 3 feet. Zones 5–10.

Blueberry Hill ('WEKcryplag')
■ *Floribunda, mauve, 1999, Carruth*
Lilac blooms (12 to 25 petals, sweet apple fragrance) and leathery dark green foliage. 3 to 4 feet. Zones 5–10. (Photo page 79.)

Brass Band ('JACcofl')
■ *Floribunda, apricot blend, 1993, Christensen, AARS*
Blooms (30 to 35 petals)—a medley of melon, peach, papaya, and apricot—have a fruity fragrance. 4 to 5 feet. Zones 5–10. (Photo page 79.)

Brilliant Pink Iceberg ('PRObril')
■ *Floribunda, pink blend, 1999, Weatherly*
Has all of the attributes of the 'Iceberg' but with a definite splash of cerise-pink blended with the creamy white. 3 to 4 feet. Zones 5–10. (Photos pages 7, 75.)

Easy Going ('HARflow')
■ *Floribunda, yellow blend, 1999, Harkness*
Descendant of Livin' Easy with peachy golden-yellow blooms (25 to 30 petals). 3 to 4 feet. Zones 5–10.

'Mlle Cecil Brunner'
■ *Polyantha, light pink, 1881, Ducher*
A classic with small silvery-pink flowers (30 petals) in large airy clusters. Spicy-sweet fragrance. 4 to 7 feet. Zones 6–10.

Sexy Rexy ('MACrexy')
■ *Floribunda, medium pink, 1984, McGredy*
Huge clusters on strong straight stems with blooms reminiscent of camellias. 4 to 5 feet. Zones 5–11. (Photos pages 6, 79.)

Sheila's Perfume ('HARsherry')
■ *Floribunda, yellow blend, 1982, Sheridan*
Exquisite blossoms (25+ petals) saturated with a rose and fruit fragrance. 3 to 4 feet. Zones 5–11. (Photos pages 7, 83.)

Sunsprite ('KORresia')
■ *Floribunda, deep yellow, 1977, Kordes*
Disease-resistant, with lasting, deep yellow blooms (25 to 30 petals). Licorice scent. 3 to 4 feet. Zones 5–11.

'The Fairy'
■ *Polyantha, light pink, 1932, Bentall*
Small soft pink florets (20 to 25 petals, mild apple scent) in large clusters. 3 to 5 feet. Zones 4–10. (Photo page 21.)

French Lace ('JAClace')
■ *Floribunda, white, 1980, Warriner, AARS*
Symmetrical flowers (30 to 35 petals) in tints of ivory, buff, and the palest apricot are similar in form and size to hybrid teas, with elegant clusters on strong, straight stems suitable for cutting. The bloom clusters have a look of antique lace. Fragrance is mild and fruity. Plants are of medium height,

3 to 4 feet tall, ideal for a border or low hedge. Flower production is excellent, and regrowth is rapid for successive bloom cycles. The foliage is glossy dark green. Zones 6 through 10.

Lavaglut ('KORlech')
■ *Floribunda, dark red, 1978, Kordes*
German-bred rose named for "lava flow" has nearly black-red to deep velvety red blooms (25 petals) in large, glowing clusters on strong stems above glossy, dark purplish-green foliage. Bloom color can withstand heat and rain without fading. Flowers are ruffled, camellia-like, and last at least 10 to 14 days. Plant grows quickly into an upright bush, 3 to 5 feet tall, with a spreading habit. Lightly scented. Zones 5 through 10.

Ortho's All-Star Miniatures and Mini-Floras

Miniatures and mini-floras provide a dynamic display of color throughout the blooming season. They are ideal for edging beds, growing in containers and rockeries, and taking indoors as potted plants. They grow 15 to 36 inches tall and bear 1- to 2-inch flowers in small to medium-sized clusters. Bloom shapes include single-petaled, rosette, or classic hybrid tea form. Bushes are rounded and dense with leaves and flowers. Mini-floras are between miniatures and floribundas in bloom size and foliage. The American Rose Society adopted this classification in 1999 to recognize another step in the evolution of the rose.

Behold ('SAVahold')

■ *Miniature, medium yellow, 1996, Saville*

Long urn-shaped buds spiral open into clear bright yellow blooms (12 to 25 petals) with a lighter reverse. Colorfast even in hot, sunny climates, the florets are in small clusters on strong stems. Flower form is the classic hybrid tea with a high center and petals unfurling in a symmetrical pattern. In spite of the low petal count, the blooms can last for weeks. The foliage is medium dull green on a vigorous, upright, small bush only 1 to 2 feet tall. Mildew is possible in coastal climates. Zones 5 through 11.

Gourmet Popcorn ('WEOpop')

■ *Miniature, white, 1986, Desamero*

A floriferous, semidouble white miniature (15 to 20 petals), consistently voted top of the list in garden display. A sport of 'Popcorn', this variety boasts pure white flowers in massive clusters, with a light fragrance, on an upright and bushy plant 2 to 3 feet tall. The growth habit is also admired for its disease-resistant, dark green foliage. This variety has received universal acceptance because of its ease of adaptation to various planting styles—it looks good in containers, in hanging baskets, and as a standard tree. It is frequently used as a border plant that contributes constant color drama throughout the year. Zones 4 through 10.

Santa Claus ('POUlclaus')

■ *Miniature, dark red, 1991, Olesen*
A Danish import with glossy dark green foliage supporting large trusses of deep scarlet blooms (15 to 25 petals). The flowers hold their color well without fading, even in midday sun. The flower form is that of the classic hybrid tea. Normally 1 to 3 feet tall, the bush can grow up to 4 feet tall in moderate climates. Best in mass plantings as a border. May be susceptible to spider mites in warm climates. Zones 5 through 10.

Rainbow's End ('SAValife')

■ *Miniature, yellow blend, 1984, Saville, AOE*
One of the most attractive miniature roses ever developed. The blooms (35 petals) start off as deep yellow with a spectacular red edging on the outer petals, deepening with age to red in the heart. As they mature each blossom becomes differently toned to create a tapestry of color. The plant is a compact, low-growing bush 12 to 18 inches tall and covered with flowers on short stems, making it ideal for containers and borders. This variety lacks fragrance, but the color show is spectacular. Zones 5 through 11.

Magic Carrousel ('MORrousel')

■ *Miniature, red blend, 1972, Moore, AOE*
One of the first miniatures to be given the ARS Award of Excellence (1975), and still adored by the rose-growing public. The double flowers are creamy white with a vivid red edge and well-formed high center. The fully open blooms reveal a dazzling, symmetrical petal arrangement contrasted with golden-yellow stamens. Plant grows 1 to 2 feet tall. Zones 4 through 11.

MORE ORTHO ALL-STAR MINIATURES AND MINI-FLORAS

Autumn Splendor ('MICautumn')

■ *Mini-flora, yellow blend, 1999, Williams, AOE*
One of the latest introductions in mini-floras, providing an explosion of changing autumn colors. Flowers are long-lasting even in heat. 2 to 3 feet. Zones 5–11. (Photo page 47.)

'Beauty Secret'

■ *Miniature, medium red, 1965, Moore, AOE*
A classic miniature from the 1960s that embodies all that is desired in a miniature rose—a small, healthy plant with low maintenance. 12 to 15 inches. Zones 4–11.

Hot Tamale ('JACpoy')

■ *Miniature, yellow blend, 1993, Zary, AOE*
Electric yellow-orange blooms age dramatically to deeper hues. The bush is low-growing and covered with flowers all season. 12 to 15 inches. Zones 5–11. (Photo page 46.)

Irresistible ('TINresist')

■ *Miniature, white, 1989, Bennett*
White blooms with a creamy center are often produced in large clusters on strong, straight stems. 2 to 3 feet. Zones 4–10. (Photo page 7.)

'Jeanne LaJoie'

■ *Climbing miniature, medium pink, 1975, Sima, AOE*
A popular climbing miniature. Can be trained to cover a fence, trellis, or arbor for a stunning display. Given space it will spread more than 10 feet. Zones 4–11. (Photos pages 11, 73.)

Jilly Jewel (BENmfig)

■ *Miniature, medium pink, 1996, Benardella*
Long shapely buds spiral open into elegant porcelain pink blooms on a medium-sized bush. The flowers are generally in large sprays. 1 to 2 feet. Zones 5–11. (Photo page 67.)

'Loving Touch'

■ *Miniature, apricot blend, 1983, Jolly, AOE*

Exceptional for its well-rounded form and its prolific display of flowers all summer. 12 to 18 inches. Zones 5–10. (Photos pages 7, 67.)

Old Glory ('BENday')

■ *Miniature, medium red, 1988, Benardella, AOE*
Stunning bright red flowers age gracefully to crimson red on a low-growing bush covered with lush, disease-resistant foliage. 12 to 18 inches. Zones 4–10.

Scentsational ('SAVamor')

■ *Miniature, mauve, 1995, Saville*
Unusual flower color in a low-spreading bush with rapid bloom repeat—and a delicious, powerful fragrance. 12 to 18 inches. Zones 5–11. (Photo page 46.)

X-Rated ('TINx')

■ *Miniature, pink blend, 1993, Bennett*
Luscious plant with creamy white flowers (blushing soft pink to coral) in clusters. Slight fragrance. 2 to 3 feet. Zones 5–10. (Photo page 91.)

Ortho's All-Star Old Garden Roses and Species

Old garden roses and species (wild) roses range from dainty to huge. They're perfect for such diverse uses as hedges, coverings for walls and arbors, fragrance gardens, borders, and flower arranging.

There are more than 200 species roses in the world, with about 35 native to the United States and Canada. Many wild roses can spread by suckering and layering 30 to 50 feet in every direction. Species roses have 5 petals; other old garden roses can be quartered, cupped, imbricated, reflexed, globular, or compact. After an initial spring bloom cycle, many varieties stop producing flowers but put on colorful displays of rose hips, which add a different kind of beauty to the garden.

The American Rose Society defines old garden roses as those existing before 1867, when the first hybrid tea was introduced. The oldest rose to be identified is *Rosa gallica*. Old garden roses, famous for their heady fragrance, are grouped into the following classes:

ALBA: Very hardy (Zone 3). Generally upright, often climbing, with dense, disease-resistant, blue-green foliage. Fragrant flowers.

AYRSHIRE: Sprawling roses that bloom once in late spring. Usually used as climbers.

BOURBON: Blooms repeatedly. Ranges from 2 to 15 feet tall in warm climates. Zones 6–10.

BOURSAULT: Rambling, thornless roses that bloom once in late spring. Hardy Zones 3–9.

CENTIFOLIA: Zones 4–9. Flowers, with 100 petals, bloom once in late spring. 4 to 8 feet.

DAMASK: Plants 3 to 6 feet tall with heavy fragrance; most bloom once, some repeatedly. Moderately hardy, Zones 6–10.

HYBRID CHINA: Small plants, 2 to 3 feet tall. Repeat blooming. Tender, Zones 7–10.

HYBRID GALLICA: Small plants 3 to 4 feet tall that bloom once in late spring. Zones 4–9.

HYBRID PERPETUAL: Plants grow 6 feet tall; flowers are fragrant and bloom repeatedly. Hardiness varies.

MOSS: Some varieties bloom repeatedly; plants grow 3 to 6 feet tall. Hardy to Zone 4.

NOISETTE: Large sprawling plants, up to 20 feet tall. Fragrant. Tender, Zones 7–11.

PORTLAND: Blooms repeatedly; 4 feet tall. Moderately hardy, Zones 6–10.

TEA: Small to medium plants, 4 to 5 feet tall, with droopy flowers that bloom repeatedly. Tender, Zones 7–11.

'Konigin von Danemark'
■ *Alba, medium pink, 1816*

Tight, stubby buds spiral open into flat flowers packed with bright, flesh pink petals, darker at the center. Large blooms, 3 to 4 inches in diameter, usually appear in heavy clusters that often bend stems to the ground. In very wet regions the blooms do not open fully, but the fragrance is exquisite. This one-season bloomer is covered with attractive, deep bluish-green leaves. Grows to 5 feet. Zones 3 through 10.

'Charles de Mills'
■ *Hybrid gallica, mauve, before 1746*

The flowers of this romantic favorite range from dark red to crimson to rich purple. Quartered in form, they can reach up to 5 inches wide, the largest of the hybrid gallicas. Flat-topped buds open into cupped blooms that quickly mature into gigantic saucer-shaped flowers. Petals are velvety. Blooms appear only once, in late spring. Susceptibility to mildew requires space around plants for air circulation. Grows 4 to 6 feet tall. Zones 4 through 10.

MORE ORTHO ALL-STAR OLD GARDEN ROSES AND SPECIES

'Baronne Prevost'
■ *Hybrid perpetual, medium pink, 1842, Desprez*
Durable rose-pink flowers (100 petals) in small clusters on strong straight stems. 3 to 6 feet. Recurrent. Zones 7–10.

'Celsiana'
■ *Damask, light pink, before 1750*
Semidouble blooms tend to nod. Strong musk fragrance. Blooms once in early summer. 3 to 4 feet. Zones 4–10.

'Harison's Yellow'
■ *Hybrid foetida, deep yellow, about 1830*
Small, spectacular, bright yellow blooms appear briefly once in spring. Attractive hips are bristly, oval, and black. The plant grows 10 to 12 feet in just a few seasons. Zones 3–9.

'Marchesa Boccella' ('Jacques Cartier')
■ *Hybrid perpetual, light pink, 1842, Desprez*
Fragrant blooms, about 3 inches wide, on tight clusters. Good repeat flowering. 3 to 4 feet. Zones 4–10.

'Mutabilis'
■ *China tea, yellow blend, before 1894*
Single-petaled flowers mature from sulfur yellow to orange, copper, red, and finally crimson, creating an artist's palette on one bush. 4 to 6 feet. Long flowering period. Zones 7–10.

'Paul Neyron'
■ *Hybrid perpetual, medium pink, 1869*
Big fragrant flowers with more than 50 petals repeat well on an upright plant that grows 4 to 5 feet. Zones 5–10. (Photo page 80.)

Rosa glauca
■ *Species, medium pink*
Small, single-petaled, starlike flowers (1 inch wide) appear once in late spring in soft lilac-pink color. Grayish purple foliage. Ideal as dense hedge. 5 to 8 feet. Zones 2–9. (Photo page 6.)

'Safrano'
■ *Tea, apricot blend, 1839*
Large, fragrant, semidouble flowers, apricot-yellow or saffron. Can tolerate some shade. 4 to 5 feet. Recurrent. Zones 7–10.

'Salet'
■ *Moss, medium pink, 1854*
Large, full, rose-pink flowers are flat, 2 to 3 inches across, and bloom intermittently. 4 to 5 feet. Zones 4–10.

'Sombreuil'
■ *Climbing tea, white, 1850, Robert*
Refined white blooms are the essence of what an old garden rose should be—flat, quilled, quartered, and double. Plants are repeat blooming. 6 to 12 feet. Zones 7–10. (Photos pages 6, 62, 80.)

Rosa Mundi
■ *Species (Rosa gallica versicolor), pink blend, before 1581*

This sport of the Apothecary's Rose is the oldest striped rose known. Its blooms are semidouble, usually 4 inches wide, with red and pink stripes against a white background, accentuated by golden-yellow stamens. No two petals are alike on the bloom. This once-blooming plant grows 3 to 4 feet tall with a sprawling habit. Suitable as a hedge plant, its branches tend to droop under the weight of the flowers and often need support. Sometimes called "Rosamund's Rose." Zones 4 through 9.

'Stanwell Perpetual'
■ *Hybrid spinosissima, white, 1838, Lee*
Has habit and foliage of a Scots Rose (small and ferny with lots of 9-leaf sets), with the repeat flowering of autumn damasks. Flowers are pale blush pink, double, quartered, and quilled, with a delicious fragrance. Canes are covered with thorns. Remove old wood each year. Grows 3 to 5 feet. Zones 3 through 9.

Apothecary's Rose
■ *Species (Rosa gallica officinalis), deep pink, before 1600*
Its semidouble blooms have four rows of petals that change gradually from bright crimson to purple with golden stamens. Intense fragrance makes petals ideal for potpourri. Fall brings lovely dark green foliage and attractive rose hips. The plant grows 3 to 4 feet tall. Once-blooming. Zones 4 through 10.

Ortho's All-Star Shrubs—Classic and Modern

Shrub is a generic classification given to a heterogeneous group of roses that don't fit neatly into any other category. Some are compact, growing no more than 3 feet tall; others sprawl to as much as 12 to 15 feet wide. What stands out about this class is its vigor, repeat cycles of bloom, disease resistance, and low maintenance. Some shrub roses make ideal hedges; others perform well as ground covers and in beds. There are five popular subdivisions—four classic and one modern—within this class.

HYBRID KORDESII: Evolutionary cross between *R. rugosa* and *R. wichuraiana*, resulting in low-growing, very hardy climbers.

HYBRID MOYESII: Tall, stiff plants with repeat bloom, followed by hips (fruits) shaped like flagons.

HYBRID MUSK: Descendants of *R. moschata*. Tall, hardy, disease-resistant, and tolerant of some shade.

HYBRID RUGOSA: Dense low-growing plants with wrinkled foliage; more tolerant of wind and rain than many other roses.

MODERN SHRUBS: The modern shrub category is known for its great diversity, versatility, and easy care in the landscape.

English roses are among the most popular modern shrub roses. Introduced by David Austin, like hybrid teas and floribundas they bloom repeatedly all summer, with many varieties possessing modern colors such as red, yellow, apricot, and salmon. Yet the flowers often have the romantic look and fragrance of old garden roses. Some have the added values of vigor, hardiness, and disease resistance. Since Austin premiered his revolutionary line of shrubs, other breeders have followed suit with equally appealing products. As a result, today you can enjoy a vast selection of modern shrubs. While some are classified as hybrid teas or floribundas, many of the Generosa and Romantica roses from France and the Renaissance roses from Denmark fall within this group.

'Belinda'
■ *Hybrid musk, medium pink, 1936, Bentall*

Small, graceful, abundant flowers are a warm shade of rosy pink with small areas of white at the base of the petals. First flush of spring brings large pyramidal clusters of 30 to 40 flowers each, on strong stems. Repeat bloom is less abundant but still fairly showy. Fragrance is light and delicate. Plant grows 4 to 6 feet tall and can be trained as a pillar rose or hedge. Foliage is a robust medium green and quite disease-resistant. Zones 5 through 9.

Knock Out ('RADrazz')
■ *Shrub, red blend, 1999, Radler, AARS*

Virtually impervious to black spot, this genetic breakthrough sets the standard for the new generation of care-free shrub roses. Its single, deep cherry red flowers (5 to 7 petals, 3 inches wide) blanket the plant in small clusters of color in spring, followed by excellent repeat bloom throughout the summer. Light tea scent. Mounded, compact plant with dense purplish-green foliage. Excellent when paired with its sister plant, Carefree Sunshine. 4 to 6 feet. Zones 4 through 10.

Abraham Darby ('AUScot')

■ *Shrub, orange pink, 1990, Austin*

One of Austin's best, with small clusters of large cupped flowers in a peachy-apricot blend. Pronounced fragrance. Foliage is shiny, healthy, and dark green. This well-disciplined, rounded bush can grow 4 to 6 feet tall—higher in warm climates. Its constant color is ideal for a country garden look. Zones 4 through 9.

'John Cabot'

■ *Hybrid kordesii, medium red, 1978, Svedja*

Semidouble, 2- to 3-inch flowers, medium red to dark orchid-pink, bloom all summer in small clusters. Have a hint of fragrance in moderate climates. Vigorous growth habit with large, arching, thorny canes; can be trained as a small 6- to 10-foot climber in warm climates or as a dense 4- to 5-foot hedge in colder areas. Dense green foliage. Needs no protection to survive harsh winters. Zones 3 through 10.

'Sally Holmes'

■ *Shrub, white, 1976, Holmes*

Can spread rapidly to reach 10 feet high and wide in warm climates. Arched canes are covered with stems bearing large clusters of blooms reminiscent of a gigantic hydrangea. Buds open into creamy white flowers that fade to pure white (creamy pink in cool climates). Fragrance is delicate, and foliage is glossy green. Repeat bloom is less spectacular than first spring flush. In warm, mild-winter climates, canes can grow to several inches in diameter. Zones 4 through 10.

MORE ORTHO ALL-STAR SHRUBS—CLASSIC AND MODERN

All That Jazz ('TWOadvance')

■ *Shrub, orange pink, 1991, Twomey, AARS*

Plants covered with attractive small sprays of semidouble coral-salmon florets with bold damask fragrance. 4 to 6 feet. Zones 5–9. (Photo page 7.)

Bonica ('MEIdomonac')

■ *Shrub, medium pink, 1985, Meilland, AARS*

Bountiful, pure rose-pink sprays of seemingly never-ending flowers. 3 to 4 feet. Zones 4–10. (Photo page 25.)

'Gartendirektor Otto Linne'

■ *Shrub, deep pink, 1934, Lambert*

Big clusters of small, old-fashioned pink blooms that repeat well. Unscented. 5 to 6 feet. Zones 4–9.

Golden Celebration ('AUSgold')

■ *Shrub, deep yellow, 1993, Austin*

Strongly scented blooms, colorfast even in strong sun. Plant needs constant grooming to maintain reasonable size. 5 to 8 feet. Zones 4–10. (Photo page 81.)

'Kathleen'

■ *Hybrid musk, light pink, 1922, Pemberton*

Richly fragrant small blooms in large clusters resemble apple blossoms. Orange hips provide a show in fall. 6 to 12 feet. Zones 5–9.

Leonard Dudley Braithwaite ('AUScrim')

■ *Shrub, dark red, 1993, Austin*

Pleasing scent from dark crimson blooms that hold well, even in heat and rain. Medium-sized plant. 4 to 6 feet. Zones 5–10. (Photo page 50.)

Mary Rose ('AUSmary')

■ *Shrub, medium pink, 1983, Austin*

Lavish display of pink blooms with hint of lavender. Damask fragrance. Medium-sized plant. 4 to 6 feet. Zones 4–11. (Photo page 54.)

Oranges 'n' Lemons ('MACoranlem')

■ *Shrub, orange blend, 1994, McGredy*

Dramatic flowers with stripes of pure yellow splashed onto bright orange. Plants can be trained as pillars or climbers 6 to 8 feet tall. Zones 4–9.

Pillow Fight ('WEKpipogop')

■ *Shrub, white, 1999, Carruth*

The first in a new generation of shrublets so thick with blooms that they conceal the foliage. 2 to 3 feet. Zones 4–9. (Photos pages 9, 66.)

'Sea Foam'

■ *Shrub, white, 1964, Schwartz*

Double flowers of glistening white. Delicate fragrance. Blooms hold up well through bad weather. A good variety to train as weeping tree rose. 2 to 8 feet. Zones 5–10.

Easiest Roses for Massing

This section addresses ways to solve familiar landscape problems with roses. For nonstop color and bloom on banks or in beds, roses can't be beat. Low-growing and wide-spreading varieties make excellent ground covers; small rounded forms are good for edging; and taller forms work well massed in large beds or in hedges.

Easiest Roses for Ground Covers

Ground-cover roses are ideal for a massed planting. They bloom over a long period of time in a wide variety of colors that stand out against attractive green leaves.

Varieties with bold-colored blooms can divide your lawn into visually separate areas. Or plant them in front of taller shrubs to heighten the interest in your borders, as well as keep down weeds.

Ground-cover roses are so tough and versatile that in some parts of the country they are used for freeway plantings. Use these roses to line paths and driveways with ribbons of color and to stabilize slopes and banks. Their spreading, shallow roots help prevent erosion while making a splash of color.

If you're planting ground-cover roses in a wide bed in front of a brick wall, consider growing a white-flowered variety such as 'White Meidiland', 'Starry Night', or 'Gourmet Popcorn' for contrast. Against a white fence, however, anything goes. Bold red, orange, or golden yellow flowers grab your attention; light and medium pink blooms harmonize with nearby pink, lavender, and blue-flowered perennials and the white fence.

For ground-cover use choose a variety with lush leaves and long, limp, narrow canes that can spread 4 to 8 feet. A single plant may eventually cover 30 to 40 square feet with a height of only 1 to 2 feet. The clustered flowers of the best ground-cover roses often last a long time and require no deadheading before each period of bloom. They work well in hard-to-reach garden spots because they require little hands-on care.

These ground-cover roses are notable for lavish blooms, disease resistance, and abundant, healthy foliage.

Royal Bonica ('MEImodac')
■ *Shrub, medium pink, 1994, Meilland*

This sport of Bonica bears rich pink flowers (15 to 25 petals, 2 inches wide) in small clusters. Fragrance is slight but stronger in cool climates. At the height of the spring flush, its prolific blossoms hide the foliage. In warmer climates bushes can grow 3 feet tall and spread about 4 feet. Set plants 6 feet apart to create a dense carpet of color. Remove spent blooms to quicken the repeat-bloom cycle. Zones 5 through 10.

Starry Night ('ORAwichkay')

■ *Shrub, white, 2002, Orard, AARS*

Among the best of the new care-free ground-cover roses. Nearly always in bloom. from late spring through fall, it bears huge clusters of single-petaled, bright white flowers (5 petals) with golden stamens reminiscent of flowering dogwood. Slight fragrance. Spreads 4 to 6 feet. Zones 4 through 10.

Electric Blanket ('KORpancom')

■ *Shrub, coral pink, 2002, Kordes*

The latest in self-maintaining ground covers. Glowing coral-pink flowers (25 to 30 petals) are borne in small clusters on short, strong stems. Foliage is glossy dark green. Repeat bloom is extremely fast. Bush spreads 3 feet across; space 4 feet apart for ground cover. Zones 4 through 10.

Red Ribbons ('KORtemma')

■ *Shrub, dark red, 1998, Kordes*

This colorful shrub requires so little care that it is used extensively in street plantings. The small flowers (17 to 25 petals, 2 inches wide), usually in small clusters, have a light, fresh scent. Plants grow about 2 to 3 feet tall and can spread 4 to 5 feet in every direction; space bushes about 8 feet apart for good coverage. The glossy bright green foliage is impervious to disease. Although you get the most bloom in the first cycle in spring, this variety reflowers reasonably well without deadheading. But if you do remove spent blooms, you will accelerate the next cycle. Zones 4 through 10.

MORE EASY ROSES FOR GROUND COVERS

These plants generally grow 2 to 3 feet tall. Space them 2 feet apart.

Aspen ('POUlurt')
■ *Shrub, medium yellow, 1995, Poulsen*
Small, semidouble, cupped flowers in elegant small clusters. Zones 4–10.

Cape Cod ('POUlfan')
■ *Shrub, light pink, 1995, Poulsen*
Large single-petaled flowers. Blooms profusely all summer. Zones 4–10.

Central Park ('POUlpyg')
■ *Shrub, apricot blend, 1995, Poulsen*
Compact clusters of warm peach flowers, yellow centers. Zones 4–10.

Cliffs of Dover ('POUlemb')
■ *Shrub, white, 1995, Poulsen*
Arched canes. Many small clusters of white blooms with golden stamens. Zones 4–10. (Photo page 11.)

First Light ('DEVrudi')
■ *Shrub, light pink, 1998, Marciel, AARS*
Small single flowers, purple stamens. Zones 5–9. (Photo page 48.)

Flower Carpet ('NOAtraum')
■ *Shrub, deep pink, 1989, Noack*
Huge clusters of deep pink flowers. 2 to 3 feet high, 4 to 5 feet wide. Zones 4–9. (Photo page 11.)

Gourmet Popcorn ('WEOpop')
■ *Miniature, white, 1986, Desamero*
Highly rated ground cover. Large clusters of white blooms. Zones 4–10. (Photos pages 9, 34.)

Napa Valley ('POUlino')
■ *Shrub, medium red, 1995, Olesen*
Bright crimson blooms on a small, compact, 2-foot plant. Zones 4–9.

Natchez ('POUllen')
■ *Shrub, medium pink, 1994, Olesen*
Abundant small blooms in dainty clusters. Easy-care. Zones 4–9.

Newport ('POUlma')
■ *Shrub, medium pink, 1994, Olesen*
Large double blooms on compact, 2- to 3-foot plant. Zones 4–10.

Pillow Fight ('WEKpipogop')
■ *Shrub, white, 1999, Carruth*
Similar to Gourmet Popcorn, with larger flowers. Honey and rose scent. Zones 4–9. (Photos pages 9, 66.)

White Meidiland ('MEIcoublan')
■ *Shrub, white, 1986, Meilland*
Large very double white blooms. 1 to 2 feet high, 4 to 5 feet wide. Zones 5 through 10. (Photo page 9.)

Easiest Roses for Beds

For a grand garden statement, fill an entire bed with many plants of one rose variety. Seen from a distance or from above, that bed will have tremendous visual impact. For an even more daring effect, select a bold-colored bedding rose in scarlet, orange, or chrome-yellow.

Traditionally the shape of rose beds is geometric—square, star-shaped, triangular, rectangular, trapezoidal, circular, or oval. Clean edges and geometric design give rose beds a formal look. To focus attention on a rose bed, locate it at the end of a garden axis, or set identical beds on either side of the axis. Make sure the beds are easy to maintain; a circular bed is easy to mow around; the sharp corners of a star can be difficult to negotiate.

Research the mature height of the roses you want to grow. If you place your rose bed against a tall yew hedge or a wall, you may want to grow taller roses in the back. If you create an island bed, taller plants will likely be in the middle. The center is an attractive place for rose trees, surrounded by miniatures or floribundas.

The bedding varieties featured here preserve their color as they age, keep flowering after the first flush of bloom, and have an appealing form or habit. Large clusters of flowers and continuous bloom maximize the bed's impact. Because blooms at many stages of maturity are on the plants together, spent blooms should not spoil the bed's overall color effect.

Floribundas, modern shrubs, and miniatures bring continuous color throughout the season by providing plentiful clusters and sprays of flowers. When planting rose bushes allow room for air circulation and access around the plants for deadheading, grooming, and cutting. The planting distance between hybrid teas, miniatures, and floribundas is about 2 feet; the space between shrub or ground-cover roses is about 3 feet. Select plants that do not set hips or fruits because they require regular deadheading. Also, choose plants that bloom all season long and don't require much grooming and attention. Keep the bed mulched to reduce weeds and to maintain moisture levels.

What a Peach ('CHEw-peach-dell')

■ *Shrub, apricot blend, 2002, Warner*
This is the latest development in small shrub roses suited for mass planting. Its flowers grow in large clusters of scrumptious, long-lasting florets, blending from deep to light peach hues. Plants grow to 3 feet tall with an upright habit. Space 2 feet apart. Foliage is glossy green, new growth is reddish plum. Mildly fruity fragrance. Zones 5 through 10.

Nicole ('KORicole')

■ *Floribunda, white, 1985, Kordes*
Large double blooms are pristine white, dramatically edged with deep cerise red. Flowers are most pleasing at the fully open stage when the golden stamens are revealed. Blooms appear in medium to large clusters on strong canes covered with many thorns. Plants are vigorous, with excellent dark green foliage. Look-alike sister seedlings include 'Raspberry Ice' and 'Hannah Gordon'. 4 to 7 feet. Zones 5 through 10.

Crimson Bouquet ('KORbeteilich')
■ *Grandiflora, dark red, 1999, Kordes*
Unlike many red roses, this recent
introduction bears flowers (30 to 35 petals)

MORE EASY ROSES FOR BEDS

Belle Story ('AUSelle')
■ *Shrub, light pink, 1985, Austin*
Large cupped flowers with yellow stamens.
4 to 6 feet. Zones 5–9.

Cotillion ('JACshok')
■ *Floribunda, mauve, 1999, Zary*
Light lavender blooms with rich, strong,
sweet fragrance. Attractive plant habit.
Long-lasting flowers have almost 40 petals.
5 to 6 feet. Zones 5–10.

Diana, Princess of Wales ('JACshaq')
■ *Hybrid tea, pink blend, 1998, Zary*
Ivory flowers with pink blush. 4 to 6 feet.
Zones 5–10. (Photos pages 28, 31.)

Francois Rabelais ('MEInusian')
■ *Floribunda, medium red, 1998, Meilland*
Old-fashioned bright red blooms all summer.
3 to 4 feet. Zones 5–10. (Photo page 55.)

Johann Strauss ('MEloffic')
■ *Floribunda, pink blend, 1994, Meilland*
Mass planting results in a multitude of old-
fashioned candy-pink blooms with a lemony
aroma that permeates the entire garden. 4 to
5 feet. Zones 5–10. (Photo page 55.)

Miami Moon
■ *Floribunda, apricot blend, 2002, Carruth*
Small clusters of ruffled shrimp-pink blooms
with a spicy fragrance. Plant 30 inches
apart. 4 to 5 feet. Zones 5–10.

Pat Austin ('AUSmum')
■ *Shrub, orange blend, 1997, Austin*
Rosettes are bright copper on inside, paler
on outside. Powerful fragrance of old rose.
5 to 6 feet. Zones 5–9. (Photo page 51.)

Purple Heart ('WEKbipuhit')
■ *Floribunda, mauve, 1999, Carruth*
Old-fashioned blooms with spicy-clove
fragrance. A must for lovers of mauve roses.
3 to 5 feet. Zones 5–10. (Photo page 74.)

Rockin' Robin ('WEKboroco')
■ *Shrub, red blend, 1999, Carruth*
Large clusters of red-, pink-, and white-
striped blooms (40 to 45 petals). 2 to 3 feet.
Zones 4–9. (Photo page 67.)

Sexy Rexy ('MACrexy')
■ *Floribunda, medium pink, 1984, McGredy*
Huge clusters on strong straight stems, with
ruffled rosettes reminiscent of camellias. 4
to 5 feet. Zones 5–11. (Photos pages 6, 79.)

that are a clear
bright red with
no blush or
darker markings.
Their abundant
small clusters will
delight you all
summer. Flower
size is largest and
petal count is
highest in cool
climates. Slight
fragrance. Like all
varieties from the
House of Kordes,
this plant's glossy,
deep green foliage
remains
remarkably
healthy. Grows
upright, 4 to 5
feet. Zones 5
through 10.

Gift of Life, Poetry in Motion ('HARelan')
■ *Hybrid tea, yellow blend, 1999, Harkness*
Soft yellow blooms
with a hint of pink
adorn long stems,
one bloom to a
stem, giving the
planting the look of
a well-arranged garden
bouquet. Fast repeat;
blooms continuously
throughout the
season. This variety
raises funds for the
Organ Donor
Program and the National Kidney
Foundation. Zones 5 through 10.

Margaret Merril ('HARkuly')
■ *Floribunda, white, 1977, Harkness*
This vigorous variety
features tough, disease-
resistant, deep green foliage
that is denser than normally
seen on a floribunda.
Flowers are a ruffled satin
white, with an intense citrus
perfume. Habit is tall and
upright. Space 30 inches
apart for mass plantings.
Flowers are exceptionally
long-lasting. Repeat bloom
is excellent. 4 to 5 feet.
Zones 5 through 11.

Easiest Roses for Hedges

Because of their thicket-like character, most rose hedges are informal. As a result they work best in large country, cottage, or suburban gardens, where the severe character of formal hedges is inappropriate. Informal hedges, by their nature, have a spreading character and are not suited for small spaces. But they are excellent choices when you want to create privacy screens or barriers, block out ugly views, or divide the garden into rooms—all with more color and interest than a formal hedge.

Informal rose hedges vary in height but tend to be between 3 and 6 feet tall. The shrubs keep their natural bushy form but are planted close enough to create a unified look. Simplicity, a medium pink floribunda, started the craze for informal rose hedges. By planting Simplicity 2 feet apart in warm climates (18 inches apart in cooler areas), you not only screen unwanted views but also give yourself a lasting source of beauty.

Hedges of shrub and floribunda roses look like thickets if you plant them close together (about 2 feet apart). Climbers, planted farther apart, give a similar but looser look.

Simplicity ('JACink')
■ *Floribunda, medium pink, 1978, Warriner*

One of the first roses developed specifically to use as a hedge, it boasts long pointed buds that open slowly to medium pink flowers (18 petals, 3 inches wide; blooms are larger in cool climates). Clusters are nearly always medium-sized and abundant in the first spring flush, providing a dazzling display for several weeks. Without deadheading, the repeat cycle is fairly fast, maintaining color from spring to fall. This variety is vigorous, hardy, and disease-resistant in all climates, although it is not a plant for severe winter climates unless protected. Light fragrance. Plants grow 4 to 5 feet tall. Zones 5 through 11.

White Simplicity ('JACsnow')
■ *Floribunda, white, 1991, Jackson & Perkins*

This variety is the next generation of Simplicity and has all the same traits. It grows 5 to 6 feet tall, blooms freely, and is tidy and self-cleaning. Double flowers— satiny white, with a touch of gold in the center when fully open—are weatherproof and can endure both strong sunshine and pouring rain. Some gardeners plant this variety along with Simplicity to give their hedges an alternating color scheme. It thrives on neglect. Plant 2 to 3 feet apart. Zones 5 through 10.

Confetti ('AROjechs')
■ *Floribunda, red blend, 1980, Swim & Christensen*

Valued for its novel colors and classic form, this variety has the fragrance of an old tea rose. Clusters of oval buds open into yellow blooms that deepen from blush to scarlet and finally to a dark red, with many colors on the bush at the same time. The flowers are long-lasting, and repeat bloom is good if spent flowers are removed regularly. Plants grow 4 to 6 feet tall with long, arching canes. Space 4 feet apart for a hedge. Zones 5 through 10.

MORE EASY ROSES FOR HEDGES

Space plants 2 to 2½ feet apart for hedges.

Bonica ('MEIdomonac')
◼ *Shrub, medium pink, 1985, Meilland, AARS*

Pure pink flowers (40+ petals) in small clusters set against rich green foliage. Blooms all season. 3 to 4 feet. Zones 4–10. (Photo page 25.)

'F.J. Grootendorst'
◼ *Hybrid rugosa, dark red, 1918, Grootendorst*

Vigorous, hardy, and disease-resistant. Unusual serrated petals, reminiscent of carnations. Zones 3–9. (Photo page 6.)

Gizmo ('WEKcatlart')
◼ *Miniature, orange blend, 1998, Carruth*

Mounded plant covererd with single-petaled blooms, scarlet-orange with white eyes. 14 to 20 inches. Zones 5–10. (Photo page 20.)

Iceberg ('KORbin')
◼ *Floribunda, white, 1958, Kordes, WFRS*

To form a dense hedge, plant these world-favorite bushes about 2 feet apart. 3 to 4 feet. Zones 5–10. (Photos pages 9, 32.)

Knock Out ('RADrazz')
◼ *Shrub, deep pink, 1999, Radler, AARS*

Vigorous shrub covered with fluorescent raspberry-red florets in medium-sized clusters. Impervious to black spot. 4 to 6 feet. Zones 4–10.

Livin' Easy ('HARwelcome')
◼ *Floribunda, orange blend, 1992, Harkness, AARS*

Apricot-orange flowers in small clusters. Can be trained to form a low hedge. 3 to 4 feet. Zones 5–10. (Photo page 32.)

Purple Simplicity ('JACpursh')
◼ *Shrub, mauve, 1998, Zary*

The latest color for the series. Deep raspberry-purple flowers hold color in hot sun. 5 to 6 feet. Zones 5–10.

Red Simplicity ('JACsimpl')
◼ *Shrub, medium red, 1991, Zary*

Brilliant, colorfast, deep red blooms (15 to 25 petals) in small clusters on a plant that needs no maintenance. 5 to 6 feet. Zones 5–10.

Sunsprite ('KORresia')
◼ *Floribunda, deep yellow, 1977, Kordes*

Classic floribunda that can be cultivated as a low-growing hcdgc. Colorfast and fragrant. 3 to 4 feet. Zones 5–11.

Betty Boop ('WEKplapic')
◼ *Floribunda, red blend, 1999, Carruth, AARS*

Eye-catching blooms (6 to 12 petals) are ivory-yellow, edged with red, in small clusters. This consistent performer in all climate zones reblooms well, even without deadheading. Rounded plant grows 3 to 5 feet tall, covered with clean glossy leaves that emerge dark red and mature to green. Plant 2 to 3 feet apart. Moderately fruity fragrance. Zones 5 through 10.

'Betty Prior'
◼ *Floribunda, medium pink, 1935, Prior*

This classic is still widely grown today for its vigor, versatility, and disease resistance. It produces immense clusters of modest-sized, single-petaled pink blooms (five petals) that age to a deeper pink. Blooming is virtually nonstop all summer— with almost no care. Grows 4 to 6 feet tall. Zones 4 through 9.

Easiest Roses for Edging

Roses are versatile. Their classic beauty makes them the main focus of mass plantings and the solitary stars of smaller gardens. Yet the same roses can take second billing to another main attraction. Small roses are perfect for edging island beds, borders, foundations, and hardscape elements such as paths, patios, driveways, and steps. Edging roses—planted close enough to visually connect—work very well at the front of a sunny bed or border, where they add a garland of color. Because of their small size, they create a transition between the lawn and garden plants. They also make good facers, covering the bare canes of hybrid teas and other leggy shrubs.

Roses used for edging should be sturdy, compact, and available in a variety of colors. Miniature roses in particular meet these requirements, and many flower all season long. The best ones for edging stand 18 to 24 inches tall. Look for compact size and color compatibility with neighboring plants. In addition to miniature roses and mini-floras, you can create a successful border by using low-growing floribundas and shrublets, which have the small size of miniatures and the vigorous habit of shrubs. These low-growers hide short weeds and fill the empty space at the base of taller plants.

For a striking effect choose an edging color that contrasts with the colors of the tall plants behind, such as a border of dark yellow Goldmarie roses edging a deep purple 'Black Knight' butterfly bush. Or plant pastels and softer hues to calm the senses. A border of Iceberg roses has twice the impact when underplanted with mauve-flowered Scentsational.

The hearty varieties listed here quickly fill their allotted space and produce a profusion of blooms.

Scentsational ('SAVamor')
■ *Miniature, mauve, 1995, Saville*
Enchanting miniature with elegant buds that open into perfectly formed blooms with a strong rose fragrance. In cool climates the mauve color deepens on the outer rim of the petals, making the blooms even more attractive. The plant is low-growing and needs little attention; in fact, it does not like severe deadheading during the growing season. Flowers are one to a stem except in warm climates, where clusters develop. Plant 12 to 18 inches apart. Zones 5 through 11.

Hot Tamale ('JACpoy')
■ *Miniature, yellow blend, 1993, Zary, AOE*
Eye-catching yellow-orange blooms age dramatically to yellow-pink, even in hot climates. Flowers are mostly one per stem; occasionally in cooler climates the plant can send up magnificent clusters of 5 to 10 florets. Blooms have a light scent and are long-lasting. Plant is compact and low-growing, 12 to 15 inches tall, densely cloaked with semiglossy dark green foliage. A recent descendant called Ruby Baby has all the same characteristics, except a deep fluorescent pink color. Plant 12 to 18 inches apart. Zones 5 through 11.

MORE EASY ROSES FOR EDGING

Height is generally 1 to 2 feet. For edging, space the following varieties 18 to 24 inches apart.

Behold ('SAVahold')
■ *Miniature, medium yellow, 1996, Saville*
Bright yellow flowers with a lighter yellow reverse. Zones 5–11. (Photo page 34.)

Figurine ('BENfig')
■ *Miniature, near white, 1991, Benardella, AOE*
Palest pink blooms look delicate but are sturdy and long-lasting. Zones 5–11.

Gizmo ('WEKcatlart')
■ *Miniature, orange blend, 1998, Carruth*
A perfectly mounded plant with abundant single-petaled blooms, scarlet-orange with a white eye. Zones 5–10.

Gourmet Popcorn ('WEOpop')
■ *Miniature, white, 1986, Desamero*
Explodes with mountains of semidouble white flowers in large sprays. Medium-sized bush. 2 to 3 feet tall. Zones 4–10. (Photos pages 9, 34.)

Kristin ('BENmagic')
■ *Miniature, red blend, 1992, Benardella, AOE*
Dramatic, deep pink edging on white petals. Zones 5–11.

Old Glory ('BENday')
■ *Miniature, medium red, 1988, Benardella, AOE*
Low-growing plant with blood red flowers of fine form. Zones 5–10.

Pillow Fight (WEKpipogop')
■ *Shrub, white, 1999, Carruth*
Stunning border plant with masses of long-lasting white blooms held in large clusters. 2 to 3 feet. Zones 4–9. (Photos pages 9, 66.)

Ralph Moore ('SAVaralph')
■ *Miniature, dark red, 2000, Saville, AOE*
Rich vibrant red blooms in small clusters; reddish-green foliage. Zones 5–10.

Sun Sprinkles ('JAChal')
■ *Miniature, deep yellow, 1999, Walden, AOE, AARS*
Colorfast yellow blooms and low-growing habit, ideal for edging. Zones 5–10.

Y2K ('SAVyk')
■ *Miniature, deep yellow, 1999, Saville*
Colorfast and fragrant with superb disease resistance. Zones 5–10.

Goldmarie ('KORfalt')
■ *Floribunda, deep yellow, 1984, Kordes*
Compact, low-growing plant ideally suited to a border. Does particularly well in warm climates. The blooms (25 to 30 petals) are a long-lasting golden color, with equally enduring golden stamens— all in large, tight clusters. In cool climates the blooms are much larger. Plants are upright, growing to a height of 24 inches, and have glossy green foliage. Fragrance is light and fruity. Repeat bloom is fast. Plant 20 to 24 inches apart. Zones 4 through 10.

Baby Love ('SCRivluv')
■ *Miniature, deep yellow, 1992, Scrivens*
This tough little shrub owes its characteristics in part to a species rose, hence its outstanding resistance to black spot. Single-petaled blooms (five petals) are sunny yellow with golden stamens. In all climates, flowers are always in bloom all summer. Mild licorice scent. Perfect for edging, this 1- to 2-foot-tall shrub can be planted as close as 12 to 15 inches around a flower bed. It retains its foliage all the way to the ground, providing an attractive backdrop for the lovely yellow flowers. Zones 4 through 11.

Autumn Splendor ('MICautumn')
■ *Mini-flora, yellow blend, 1999, Williams, AOE*
Spectacular color combination. Small to medium sprays of flowers with brilliant yellow, gold, and orange, occasionally splashed with a touch of red. Petals reflex (curl back) like a hybrid tea for elegant form and shape. As blooms age the amount of orange can dramatically increase. Plants are generally taller than their miniature cousins, reaching 30 inches. This is the first mini-flora to receive the ARS Award of Excellence. Zones 5 through 11.

Easiest Roses for the Country Look

Easiest Roses for Mixed Borders

Mixed borders combine many kinds of plants into a harmonious and unified whole. Trees, shrubs, bulbs, annuals, and perennials can work together to create colorful, long-lasting beauty. By definition, a border is a planting that grows against a hedge, wall, fence, or other backdrop, capable of being seen from just one side.

Roses fit well in mixed borders, especially those with long seasons of bloom. Upright varieties are useful where you want to create a tightly woven tapestry of colors. Yet the rounded profiles of once-blooming shrub roses work well too. Even when out of bloom, they still add calm spots between areas of color.

In a border, the tallest plants often stand at the back, the shorter ones in front. But a well-placed rose tree can create the perfect accent—in front or midborder—where its unusual form and lovely blooms can stand out.

Mixing border colors requires some planning. Use mostly warm colors in some areas, cool colors in others. Warm, intense colors—shades of red, orange, and yellow— are attention grabbers and look wonderful in sunny spots at midday (when lighter colors look washed out). Cool colors, whites, and pastels—pink, lemon-yellow, lavender, and blue—have a calming effect and appear to make the garden bigger. They also capture the light in the shaded areas you want to be seen at dusk. Pale yellows and white actually glow in the moonlight.

Astride Lindgren
■ *Shrub, light pink, 1991, Poulsen*
Large clusters of double, cupped, porcelain-pink flowers appear continuously throughout the growing season. A dense compact bush, 3 to 4 feet tall in warm climates. Sprays are excellent as cut flowers. Zones 4 through 9.

First Light ('DEVrudi')
■ *Shrub, light pink, 1998, Marciel, AARS*
Delicate single-petaled solid-pink blooms with contrasting burgundy stamens resemble an azalea in full bloom. Scent is mild and spicy. Compact rounded plant presents a natural wild-rose effect on a modern, repeat-blooming shrub. 3 to 4 feet. Zones 5 through 9.

Singin' in the Rain ('MACivy')

■ *Floribunda, apricot blend, 1994, McGredy, AARS*

Superb, unusual color makes this variety a good choice for a mixed border. Clusters of flowers (25 to 30 petals) are apricot-copper to cinnamon-apricot-gold. The plant is upright with dark green foliage. Sweet musk fragrance. 3 to 4 feet. Zones 5 through 11.

Sun Flare ('JACjam')

■ *Floribunda, medium yellow, 1981, Warriner, AARS*

A classic with lots of colorfast bright lemon blooms (20 to 30 petals) in small clusters (from 3 to as many as 15 florets) on a low, mounded bush. Fragrance is light licorice. Glossy green leaves are small and disease-free. 3 to 4 feet. Zones 5 through 10.

Bill Warriner ('JACsur')

■ *Floribunda, orange pink, 1998, Zary*

Well-spaced clusters of blooms in shades of salmon, orange, and coral with a pleasant, light fragrance. The flowers are larger than those of most floribundas, especially in cooler areas. The plant grows 4 to 5 feet tall in moderate climates. Dense foliage is glossy dark green. Zones 5 through 10.

MORE EASY ROSES FOR MIXED BORDERS

Amber Queen ('HARroony')
■ *Floribunda, apricot blend, 1983, Harkness, AARS*
Apricot-golden blooms (25 to 30 petals) with a sweet-spicy scent. Glossy green leaves. 2 to 3 feet. Zones 5–10. (Photo page 26.)

'Angel Face'
■ *Floribunda, mauve, 1968, Swim & Weeks, AARS*
Low-growing plant with fragrant ruffled blooms in clusters. 2 to 3 feet. Zones 5–10.

Betty Boop ('WEKplapic')
■ *Floribunda, red blend, 1999, Carruth, AARS*
Clusters of ivory flowers edged in red with golden centers. 4 to 5 feet. Zones 5–10. (Photo page 45.)

'Betty Prior'
■ *Floribunda, medium pink, 1935, Prior*
Large clusters of small single-petaled cerise-pink blooms all summer. Tea fragrance. 4 to 6 feet. Zones 4–9. (Photo page 45.)

Intrigue ('JACum')
■ *Floribunda, mauve, 1982, Warriner, AARS*
Small clusters of exotic mauve blooms with intense fragrance. 3 to 4 feet. Zones 5–10. (Photo page 7.)

Margaret Merril ('HARkuly')
■ *Floribunda, white, 1977, Harkness*
Ruffled semidouble satin blooms (28 petals) with a strong citrus scent. 4 to 5 feet. Zones 5–11. (Photo page 43.)

'Nearly Wild'
■ *Floribunda, medium pink, 1941, Brownell*
Single-petaled blooms with a whitish eye cover the entire bush in spring. Apple fragrance. 2 to 3 feet. Zones 4–9. (Photo page 56.)

Pillow Fight ('WEKpipogop')
■ *Shrub, white, 1999, Carruth*
Massive clusters of double flowers on a small shrublet. 2 to 3 feet. Zones 4–9. (Photos pages 9, 66.)

'The Fairy'
■ *Polyantha, light pink, 1932, Bentall*
Small ruffled florets (20 to 25 petals, mild apple scent) in large pyramidal clusters. 3 to 5 feet. Zones 4–9. (Photo page 21.)

Easiest Roses for Companion Planting

There are two main reasons for combining roses with other plants. First, companion plants can bring color and texture to stretches of green rose foliage between bloom cycles—or hide bare brown stems in spring. Second, the leaves or flowers of some companion plants enhance the beauty of blooming roses by harmonizing or contrasting with their colors.

For an early display in the shrub border, combine azaleas, lilacs, and viburnums with your later-blooming roses. Shrubs such as hydrangeas that hold dried flowers through winter can extend the interest in the shrub border well beyond the roses' last bloom. Likewise, when rose beds look bare and lifeless in spring, an underplanting of early bulbs such as snowdrops, crocus, squill, glory-of-the-snow, or daffodils adds color and life.

Traditional companions for roses include fragrant herbs such as lavender, catmint, and thyme. These pairings date from the days when roses were considered herbs and had medicinal value. The fragrant gray-green leaves and purple flowers of catmint and lavender look handsome with roses, and they cover the sometimes naked legs of these flowering shrubs. Another classic companion is large-flowered hybrid clematis, a small vine that is light and open enough to not smother rose bushes. You can plant clematis vines, which come in numerous colors—from pink and purple to white and yellow—to scramble through your rosebushes, creating harmonies of color and form as they go. Because some clematis bloom when your roses don't, they add a second season of showy flowers.

Color is a key factor. For example, blue flowers, such as delphinium or 'Butterfly Blue' pincushion flower, will make pale mauve roses appear washed out. Conversely, white-flowered companions such as some peonies or shasta daisies can act as an attractive buffer between strong-colored groupings of red, yellow, or orange roses.

Evelyn ('AUSsaucer')

■ *Shrub, apricot blend, 1992, Austin*
Large apricot-yellow flowers with more than 40 petals are shallow-cupped, gradually building to a beautiful rosette shape at maturity. In warm-weather climates the color is more pink than apricot. Very prominent fragrance. Vigorous, upright-growing, 4- to 6-foot bush blooms constantly. Underplant with 6-inch-tall *Nepeta* 'Blue Wonder' or 18-inch *N.* 'Dropmore', which can be sheared back by half in midseason for a second flush of bloom. Zones 5 through 10.

Leonard Dudley Braithwaite ('AUScrim')

■ *Shrub, dark red, 1993, Austin*
Red-to-crimson blooms are symmetrical and round, with petals gently folded inward in the center. Flowers are one to a stem, with some clustering in cool climates. Weather-resistant blossoms last a long time on the bush or as cut flowers. Fragrance is strong yet pleasing. Grows 4 to 6 feet tall. Plant with baby's breath—*Gypsophila* 'Bristol Fairy' or *G.* 'Compacta Plena'—for a classic florist's look. Zones 5 through 10.

Pat Austin ('AUSmum')

■ *Shrub, orange blend, 1997, Austin*

Large double blooms are a vivid combination of colors from rich copper on the topside to pale coppery yellow on the underside. They exude a fruity old-rose fragrance. Because of this plant's spreading habit, keep it about 3 feet from adjacent plants. It grows 5 to 6 feet tall. Use 30-inch *Nigella damascena* 'Oxford Blue' (Love-in-a-mist), an annual with large, double blue flowers, to set off the coppery roses. Sow every two weeks from early spring to midsummer. *Nigella* may self-sow the following spring. Zones 5 through 9.

Geoff Hamilton ('AUSham')

■ *Shrub, medium pink, 1999, Austin*

This modern shrub looks like an old garden rose and is very resistant to disease. Crowded petals infold to produce an attractive quartered bloom. Flowers are a rose-pink with the outer petals fading to white. Fragrance is strong. Both the plant and its flowers perform best in warm climates; rain and wind can damage stems. Grows 4 to 6 feet tall with matte light green foliage. Underplant it with *Clematis* 'Perle d'Azur' and let this small blue-flowered vine clamber up through the canes. Zones 5 through 10.

Gertrude Jekyll ('AUSbord')

■ *Shrub, medium pink, 1986, Austin*

Its rich, glowing pink blossoms are informal perfect spheres on straight stems. In cool climates where it can get tall (5 to 6 feet) and somewhat lanky, this rose looks best if kept to a height of about 2 to 3 feet in a mixed border. Its attractive grayish leaves and all-summer blooms work well with *Gaura lindheimeri* 'Siskiyou Pink', which produces wands of pretty pink flowers that weave through the stems of the rose all season long. Or use species gaura's pale pink blooms for a wispy look. Zones 5 through 10.

MORE EASY ROSES FOR COMPANION PLANTING

Ambridge Rose ('AUSwonder')

■ *Shrub, apricot blend, 1994, Austin*

Large cupped blooms are rich apricot touched with gold. Strong stems. 4 to 6 feet. Zones 4–10.

English Garden ('AUSbuff')

■ *Shrub, apricot blend, 1990, Austin*

Double old-fashioned blooms with a delicate apricot-yellow at the center, fading to yellow at the edges. 4 to 5 feet. Zones 4–9. (Photo page 26.)

Fair Bianca ('AUSca')

■ *Shrub, white, 1983, Austin*

Fully double, cupped, pure white flowers with attractive small green pip in center. Strong myrrh aroma. 4 to 5 feet. Zones 5–9.

Golden Celebration ('AUSgold')

■ *Shrub, deep yellow, 1993, Austin*

Cupped blooms are more golden than most yellow roses. Strong fragrance. 5 to 8 feet. Zones 4–10. (Photo page 81.)

Redoute ('AUSpale')

■ *Shrub, light pink, 1994, Austin*

Old-fashioned, soft, delicate pink blooms in smallish clusters on upright plant. 4 to 5 feet. Zones 5–9.

The Prince ('AUSvelvet')

■ *Shrub, dark red, 1993, Austin*

Royal purple to dark red flowers (100 petals, 4 inches wide, heavy old-rose perfume). 2 to 3 feet. Zones 4–9.

Easiest Companion Plants for Roses

Traditional cottage gardens mix roses with many other flowers. The finished look is cheerful and fun, a hodgepodge of plants that sometimes stretch, sprawl, and self-sow within the confines of well-edged beds. To create a cottage garden in your yard, you don't have to use old-fashioned flowers, though many complement the shape and blooms of today's hardiest and healthiest shrub roses. Just be sure that the flowers you choose enhance the look of your roses or extend the season of bloom for your garden. Remember that the foliage of a perennial is almost more important than its flowers, because the flowers typically last just two to three weeks. Many annuals, on the other hand, provide season-long color for a mixed border or cottage garden. The following list includes both annual and perennial flowers that thrive with roses in many parts of the country.

TOP COMPANIONS FOR ROSES

■ *Clematis* **hybrids (large-flowered clematis)**
This deciduous, woody vine grows 5 to 8 feet per year. Its big, dramatic blooms and showy seed heads look attractive interspersed throughout rosebushes. Experiment with color. Plant pink-and-white-striped 'Nelly Moser' so it can scramble over a reblooming pink rosebush, or plant violet-purple C. × *jackmanii* with white Iceberg roses. Zones 3 through 8.

■ *Gaura lindheimeri* **(gaura)**
A short-lived perennial with a see-through habit, growing 3 to 4 feet tall and 1 to 2 feet wide. Place it in front of roses so its airy, pale pink flower spikes can weave through the roses' dense prickly stems. For a more potent effect, choose 'Siskiyou Pink', with its bright rosy pink flowers and 2- to 3-foot height, or 'Corrie's Gold', which has golden variegated foliage and pink blooms and stands 3 feet tall. Zones 5 through 8.

■ *Geranium sanguineum* **(bloody cranesbill)**
This long-lived perennial, about 12 inches tall and 18 inches wide, makes an outstanding ground cover under rosebushes by forming tidy, spreading clumps. It has red autumn leaves and magenta flowers from early summer to fall. G. *sanguineum var. striatum*, a 6- to 8-inch-tall variety, produces light pink flowers streaked with tiny veins of red. G. *macrorrhizum* is another species with magenta flowers and a spreading habit so dense that weeds can't penetrate the fleshy, aromatic network. Zones 3 through 8.

MORE EASY COMPANION PLANTS FOR ROSES

■ *Dianthus deltoides* (cottage pink)
A perennial that grows 10 inches tall and 18 inches wide, covered with fragrant pink flowers spring through frost. A refined ground cover in the rose bed. Zones 3–8.

■ *Diascia* species (twinspur)
A tender perennial, usually grown as an annual in cooler climates. Grows 10 inches tall and 12 inches wide, covered with lacy pink flowers spring through fall. Zones 7–9.

■ *Digitalis purpurea* (foxglove)
Its tall nodding spikes of tubular flowers contrast with the rounder bloom and habit of roses. Stands 4 feet tall and 3 feet wide. A biennial that will self-sow in Zones 4–9.

■ *Heliotropium arborescens* (garden heliotrope)
An annual with intense blue flower clusters, deliciously fragrant. Ideal backdrop for pink, white, red, or yellow roses. Grows 12 to 24 inches tall and 12 inches wide. Zones 5–10.

■ *Lavandula angustifolia* (lavender)
A perennial with fragrant silver foliage. Attracts bees with its perfumed purple flower spikes. Measures about 1 foot tall and 3 feet wide. Zones 5–9.

■ *Lobularia maritima* (sweet alyssum)
Annual ground cover 4 inches tall and 10 inches loaded from spring to frost with lavender, pink, or white blooms. Handsome self-sowing mat under roses. Zones 4–10.

■ *Malva alcea* (hollyhock mallow)
Flowers freely, producing pink blooms from summer to frost on sturdy stems perfect for cutting. 3 feet tall, 2 feet wide. Zones 4–8.

■ *Nigella damascena* (love-in-a-mist)
Prolific, self-sowing, 18-inch by 18-inch annual with blue flowers, attractive seedpods, see-through foliage. Zones 5–10.

■ *Paeonia* hybrids (herbaceous peony)
Three-foot perennial with fragrant flowers about the same time as old garden roses. Double-flowered peonies are lovely next to roses of similar height and color. Zones 3–8.

■ *Stachys byzantina* 'Helen von Stein' (lamb's ear)
Silvery leaves twice as big as regular lamb's-ears. Although it does well in hot climates, it also thrives in the North. Grows 12 inches tall and wide. Zones 4–9.

■ *Gypsophila paniculata* (baby's breath)
Baby's breath grows about 3 feet tall and wide. Its delicate stems are loaded with tiny, billowing white blooms. 'Bristol Fairy' has double white flowers and is 2 to 3 feet tall. 'Flamingo' can grow up to 3 feet tall and bears a profusion of double pink flowers. Zones 3 through 7.

■ *Nepeta* × *faassenii* (catmint)
Catmint grows about 18 inches tall and wide and produces bushy, aromatic gray-green leaves and abundant spikes of fragrant lavender-blue flowers for much of the summer. When massed it's a welcome contrast to the sometimes sparse-blooming second flush of a rose. 'Six Hills Giant' is tall and hardy with dark violet-blue flowers; 'Blue Wonder' measures 12 to 15 inches tall and produces 6-inch blue flower spikes. Zones 3 through 8.

Easiest Roses for Cottage Gardens

The rose is a staple of cottage garden design. Whether it's a five-petaled variety collected from a wayside near your house, a rose tree set amidst hollyhocks and foxgloves by the garden path, or a rambler smothering the wall and arbor over your front door, at least one rose is necessary for a cottage garden effect.

Today's cottage gardens draw upon the informality of ancient English models but emphasize the looks of plants over their medicinal or culinary purposes. A cottage garden can be as simple as a fragrant old garden rose such as 'Paul Neyron' set among pansies, or as complicated as fully developed mixed borders featuring heirloom plants chosen to bloom over an extended time. A cottage garden should look spontaneous—a place where self-sowing annuals abound and spreading roses are at home. Yet even this garden has an internal, though not very noticeable, structure. Achieving a balance between good form and haphazard abundance requires thought and care, making a cottage garden a challenge if your goal is a garden that's easy to maintain.

Two cottage garden designs prevail. One flanks a straight path to the front door with colorful mixed borders filled with roses, herbs, native plants, aromatic flowers, and some well-tended fruiting shrubs and trees. The other design flourishes at the back or side of the house. The big, fragrant roses listed here look good in either setting.

Mary Rose ('AUSmary')
■ *Shrub, medium pink, 1983, Austin*
Strong rose-pink blooms in tight clusters perch on slightly arching stems. In warm climates the petals shed a few days after the blooms fully open. Strong old-fashioned rose scent. Bush is exceptionally vigorous and disease-resistant, growing 4 to 6 feet tall and covered with blooms. Zones 4 through 11.

'Just Joey'
■ *Hybrid tea, orange blend, 1972, Cants, WFRS*
Large, ruffled, loose double flowers are a rich apricot blend (deeper in cool climates). Long-lasting blooms have a fruity fragrance. Foliage is lush and glossy green. The plant is a top performer in a cottage garden setting; its combination of flower size, richness of color, and informal bloom shape makes this variety unlike any other. Grows 5 to 6 feet tall. Zones 5 through 10.

MORE EASY ROSES FOR COTTAGE GARDENS

Amber Queen ('HARroony')
■ *Floribunda, apricot blend, 1983, Harkness, AARS*
Apricot-golden-yellow flowers (30 petals) in small clusters. Fast repeat bloom cycle. Superb glossy green foliage. 2 to 3 feet. Zones 5–10. (Photo page 26.)

Constance Spry ('AUSfirst')
■ *Shrub, light pink, 1961, Austin*
Soft luminous pink flowers with delicious scent of myrrh on large sprawling plant. 4 to 8 feet. Zones 4–9. (Photo page 82.)

Fair Bianca ('AUSca')
■ *Shrub, white, 1983, Austin*
Double, cupped, pure white flowers with small central green pip. Myrrh fragrance. 4 to 5 feet. Zones 5–9.

French Lace ('JAClace')
■ *Floribunda, white, 1980, Warriner, AARS*
Outstanding pastel rose. Beautifully formed blooms (30 petals). Fruity fragrance. 3 to 4 feet. Zones 6–10. (Photos pages 33, 69.)

Sexy Rexy ('MACrexy')
■ *Floribunda, medium pink, 1984, McGredy*
Huge sprays of up to 35 rosettes on strong stems. 4 to 5 feet. Zones 5–11. (Photos pages 6, 79.)

Sunset Celebration ('FRYxotic')
■ *Hybrid Tea, apricot blend, 1999, Fryer, AARS*
Rich peach blooms (35 to 40 petals). Leathery medium green foliage. 5 to 6 feet. Zones 5–10. (Photo page 24.)

Sunsprite ('KORresia')
■ *Floribunda, deep yellow, 1977, Kordes*
A classic. Flowers form in small fragrant clusters. Fairly fast repeat. 3 to 4 feet. Zones 5–11.

What a Peach ('CHEwpeachdell')
■ *Shrub, apricot blend, 2002, Warner*
Warm apricot blooms with moderately fruity scent. 2 to 3 feet. Zones 5–10. (Photo page 42.)

Y2K ('SAVyk')
■ *Miniature, deep yellow, 1999, Saville*
Colorfast blooms with good fragrance. Superb disease resistance. Small and compact. 12 to 15 inches. Zones 5–10. (Photo page 91.)

Francois Rabelais ('MEInusian')
■ *Floribunda, medium red, 1998, Meilland*
This new-era variety combines the best of old-fashioned quartered flower form with a modern plant habit, superior recurrent bloom, and compact size. Blooms (80+ petals), the color of red wine, have a slight fragrance of cedar. Massive clusters last several weeks to a month on the bush. Plants grow 3 to 4 feet tall. Zones 5 through 10.

Johann Strauss ('MEIoffic')
■ *Floribunda, pink blend, 1994, Meilland*
Exuding a delicious lemon scent with hints of apple, the large very full flowers (100+ petals) of this Romantica series rose are candy pink with an old-fashioned, globular form. The plant is upright, 4 to 5 feet high, and its medium-sized clusters display excellent repeat bloom. Superb bronze-green foliage. Zones 5 through 10.

Peter Mayle ('MEIzincaro')
■ *Hybrid tea, deep pink, 2001, Meilland*
Huge flowers on strong straight stems towering above the garden. Striking red blooms (30 to 35 petals) are symmetrical and colorfast. This is one of the most fragrant in the Romantica series offered by this famous French rose breeder. Its petals survive even the hottest summers. Plants grow 4 to 6 feet tall and are covered with attractive dark green foliage. Cut flowers are excellent for their fragrance and lasting qualities. Zones 5 through 10.

Easiest Roses for the Wild Garden

Some gardeners impose their will upon the land, filling in low spots, flattening hummocks, and pruning sprawling plants into tidy, formal balls. Other gardeners take a different approach, looking to nature for inspiration and following her guidance in shaping the land and choosing plants. Human hands work subtly in a wild garden, allowing plants to achieve their natural shape. Local materials form paths and walls, and plants suit the site, looking like natives even if they're not. Although species roses work well in the wild garden, many modern shrub roses with single-petaled flowers do even better, providing a naturalistic effect with superior reblooming and a neater habit.

When selecting roses for your wild garden, take care to choose colors and flower forms that you enjoy. Pay attention to growth habit; some varieties will form rounded bushes and others will take over the neighborhood. The thorny canes and fast-spreading habit of *R. rugosa*, a liability near the house, make it outstanding as a barrier hedge on your property line. *R. glauca* is a tamer plant with four-season appeal. Its leaves are a handsome gray-blue, its flowers single and pink. It produces reddish-orange hips after the flowers and, when the leaves fall, its arching 6-foot canes have a decorative purple cast.

Rosa rugosa rubra
■ *Species, mauve, before 1854*

Large single (five-petaled) flowers are magenta-purple, with contrasting golden stamens. Scented flowers appear one to a stem, or occasionally in small clusters, from early spring through summer. Autumn brings a lavish display of large, round, tomato red hips. This dense shrub can reach 8 feet in height. Prickly canes are covered with fawn brown thorns. Foliage features seven to nine wrinkled leaflets that are semiglossy and dark green. *R. rugosa alba* is the botanical form with pure white flowers. Zones 2 through 9.

'Nearly Wild'
■ *Floribunda, medium pink, 1941, Brownell*

Massive quantities of single-petaled pink blooms with a whitish eye cover this 2- to 3-foot-tall plant in the first spring flush of bloom. Distinct apple fragrance. Superb in cold-winter areas. Can suffer from occasional black spot if too crowded. For top performance, give plants plenty of space for air circulation. Zones 4 through 9.

Escapade ('HARpade')

■ *Floribunda, mauve, 1967, Harkness*

Large sprays of semidouble flowers (12 petals) are profuse throughout the growing season. Blooms tend to fade rather quickly in hot climates; in cool climates, color contrasts are dramatic. Quantity of nectar produced by blooms attracts honeybees. Plants are low-growing, 2 to 4 feet tall; dense foliage is glossy and light green. Excellent in the mixed herbaceous border. Zones 4 through 10.

'Morden Snowbeauty'

■ *Shrub, white, 1998, Agriculture Canada*

Capable of withstanding very cold winters. Pure white flowers are single-petaled and borne in clusters throughout the summer. Superior hardiness; excellent resistance to black spot. 3 to 4 feet. Zones 3 through 9.

Carefree Delight ('MEIpotal')

■ *Shrub, pink blend, 1994, Meilland, AARS*

Small single-petaled blooms (five petals)—carmine-pink with a white eye—grow in large clusters (10 to 15 florets per stem), covering the surface of the bush when in full flush. Unscented. Bright orange hips in winter. Extremely vigorous plant (4 to 5 feet tall) spreads a little wider than most shrub roses. Can be trained as small climber. Exceptional resistance to all fungal diseases. Very hardy; needs no winter protection. Zones 4 through 10.

MORE EASY ROSES FOR THE WILD GARDEN

Antique Artistry ('CLEartful')
■ *Floribunda, apricot blend, 2000, Clements*
Old-fashioned blooms of rich apricot-peach. Lovely damask fragrance. 4 to 6 feet. Zones 4–10.

Baby Love ('SCRivluv')
■ *Miniature, deep yellow, 1992, Scrivens*
Buttercup yellow, five-petaled blooms in small clusters. Sweet apple fragrance. 1 to 2 feet. Zones 4–11. (Photo page 47.)

Constance Finn ('HAReden')
■ *Floribunda, light pink, 1997, Harkness*
Old-fashioned blooms (50 petals) reminiscent of pink cake icing. 4 to 6 feet. Zones 5–9.

Jacqueline de Pre ('HARwanna')
■ *Shrub, white, 1988, Harkness*
Clusters of semidouble milk white blooms with rich ruby-wine stamens. Musk fragrance. 4 to 6 feet. Zones 4–9.

Johann Strauss ('MEIoffic')
■ *Floribunda, pink blend, 1994, Meilland*
Candy pink blooms (100 petals) in small clusters. Enchanting apple fragrance. 4 to 5 feet. Zones 5–10. (Photo page 55.)

Mountbatten ('HARmantelle')
■ *Floridunda, medium yellow, 1982, Harkness*
Clusters of fully double primrose yellow blooms sometimes edged with pink. 4 to 5 feet. Zones 4–10.

'Mutabilis'
■ *China tea, yellow blend, before 1894*
Single-petaled flowers mature from sulfur yellow to orange, copper, red, and finally crimson. 4 to 6 feet. Zones 7–10.

Peter Beales ('CLEexpert')
■ *Shrub, medium red, 2000, Clements*
Clusters of rich crimson-red blooms (five petals) with a golden yellow eye. 4 to 5 feet. Zones 4–10.

Peter Mayle ('MEIzincaro')
■ *Hybrid tea, deep pink, 2001, Meilland*
Very fragrant. Well-formed blooms (30 to 35 petals) on long stems, good for cutting. 4 to 6 feet. Zones 5–10.

The Easiest Climbing Roses

Easiest Climbers For Fences

Climbing roses add height and density to a garden. The long, flexible canes of the same climbers and ramblers, when trained to a vertical support, bring their flowers to eye level, where you can easily enjoy them. Climbing roses can enhance a plain brick or dry-stone wall and cover an unsightly chain link or barbed-wire fence, transforming utilitarian eyesores into objects of natural beauty.

Climbers reach a height and width of 4 to 10 feet; ramblers grow 20 to 30 feet in every direction. Their long canes bloom at almost

every leaf junction, blanketing them with flowers and making them ideal for training over walls and along fences.

Training is the key word here; long-caned roses are not vines and do not climb. Left to themselves they would mound and sprawl. When you train a rose to cover a long, low wall, choose the same variety to repeat over the length of the wall. Space climbers 5 to 6 feet apart; ramblers need even more room. Spacing the plants is crucial for success, because adjacent plants should interlock their canes to provide a uniform, hedgelike final structure.

There are several ways to train a rose on a wall. The simplest is to attach a trellis to the underlying support. A trellis has the advantage of holding the rose away from the wall so air can circulate around the canes to prevent disease. However, its disadvantage is that it shows. To help hide it paint the trellis the color of the supporting wall or a blackish-green. Or you can train the rose on heavy wire fed through eye screws attached to the wall in a vertical, horizontal, or fan-shaped pattern. The wires should be anchored to the wall every couple of feet and pulled taut. Tie the stems to the wires with flexible fabric, garden twine, or raffia, all of which will eventually disintegrate. For a healthy plant keep the canes separate; crossed or rubbing canes are vulnerable to disease.

Blaze Improved ('Blaze')
■ *Climber, medium red, 1932, Kallay*
Produces summer-long abundance of solid scarlet red flowers (20 to 25 petals) in large clusters on strong stems all along the length of its thick canes. Blooms have a light tea fragrance. Canes generally grow 12 to 14 feet long; for dense growth, space plants 7 to 8 feet apart. Train canes early to horizontal positions at various heights. Zones 5 through 10.

MORE EASY CLIMBERS FOR FENCES

Space the following varieties 5 to 6 feet apart for planting along fences and low walls.

Angel Face, Climbing
■ *Climbing floribunda, mauve, 1981, Haight*
Small climber with magnificent display of mauve flowers all summer. Zones 5–10.

'Autumn Sunset'
■ *Shrub, apricot blend, 1986, Lowe*
Warm apricot-gold blooms (20 to 25 petals) exude strong, fruity fragrance. Excellent resistance to black spot. Zones 5–10.

First Prize, Climbing ('JACclist')
■ *Climbing hybrid tea, pink blend, 1976, Reasoner*
Huge blooms (20 to 30 petals) have a lighter silvery-pink reverse. Zones 6–9.

Flutterbye ('WEKplasol')
■ *Floribunda, yellow blend, 1999, Carruth*
Single-petaled blooms—yellow, coral, tangerine, and pink. Zones 5–9.

Handel ('MACha')
■ *Climber, red blend, 1965, McGredy*
Blooms are white edged with red. Dark olive foliage. Zones 5–9. (Photo page 7.)

'Henry Kelsey'
■ *Hybrid kordesii, medium red, 1984, Svedja*
Clusters of bright red flowers. Very hardy. 6 to 8 feet. Zones 3–9. (Photo page 65.)

'Iceberg, Climbing'
■ *Climbing floribunda, white, 1968, Cant*
Classic white with abundant blooms all season long. 6 to 12 feet. Zones 5–10.

'Jeanne LaJoie'
■ *Climbing miniature, medium pink, 1975, Sima, AOE*
Small double pink flowers. Canes spread 10 feet. Zones 4–11. (Photos pages 11, 73.)

'Mlle Cecile Brunner, Climbing'
■ *Climbing polyantha, light pink, 1894, Hosp*
Large airy clusters of small pointed buds open to creamy, pale pink blooms. Canes can grow to 20 feet. Zones 6–9.

'Royal Gold'
■ *Climber, medium yellow, 1957, Morey*
Vigorous plant produces quantities of golden-yellow flowers on stems long enough for cutting. Zones 5–9.

'Joseph's Coat'
■ *Climber, red blend, 1969, Armstrong & Swim*

Hues ranging through red, pink, orange, and yellow in abundant flower clusters with light tea scent. Foliage is glossy apple green. Canes average 8 to 10 feet long. Space 5 to 6 feet apart against wall or along fence for best effect. Needs protection in harsh winter climates. Zones 5 through 10.

'Royal Sunset'
■ *Climber, apricot blend, 1960, Morey*
Blooms can be high-centered or cupped (30 to 35 petals), with a rich, fruity fragrance. Deep apricot color fades as blossoms mature to light peach color in midsummer heat; blossoms can appear a bit blowsy at times. Repeat flowering is excellent. Leathery foliage is dark copper-green. Canes grow 8 to 10 feet long. For best canopy density along fence, plant 6 feet apart. Zones 5 through 10.

'Don Juan'
■ *Climber, dark red, 1958, Malandrone*
Velvety double dark red blooms (30 to 35 petals) with strong rose fragrance cover plant all summer; small bloom clusters are perfect for cutting. Warm night temperatures produce best color. Foliage is glossy dark green. Canes can grow as much as 12 to 14 feet long, though the average length is

8 to 10 feet. Plant bushes 6 feet apart along a fence or wall for best effect. Repeat cycle is fast. Plant can suffer from frost damage during cold winters but recovers fairly fast. Zones 5 through 10.

Polka ('MEItosier')
■ *Climber, apricot blend, 1996, Meilland*
Large fluffy old-fashioned flowers (30 to 35 petals), one to a stem or in small clusters on strong stems. Dramatic copper-salmon fading to light salmon-pink with deep-copper at center. Ideal cut flowers. Fragrance strong and pervading. Plants grow 10 to 12 feet tall in most climates, with healthy-looking dark green foliage. Zones 5 through 10.

Easiest Climbers for Pillars and Posts

Rose pillars make a big impression in a small space. One 6-foot freestanding post in rot-resistant wood or reinforced concrete, planted with roses, adds significant height and architectural form to flower beds and borders. Tripods and wrought-iron posts have a similar structural presence, as do porch posts, lampposts, and mailboxes. Whatever the underlying structure the rose foliage will completely hide it after a few growing seasons.

Not all climbers flower on a pillar. Most climbers bloom profusely only when the canes are horizontal. But pillar roses are climbers that bloom freely at the leaf nodes when trained on a vertical plane. Trained pillar-rose canes should resemble a spiral staircase that loops around a central post until it reaches its final height. Direct the long, flexible canes in an ascending spiral, spaced evenly apart around the column. By intertwining the canes, you create a solid visual mass along the post. To keep the canes in place, use flexible fabric, garden twine, or raffia attached to hooks or bolts in the structure. As the rose canes grow, you may need to trim some side stems to preserve the columnar effect. Cut back stout side stems by two-thirds and weaker side stems by three-fourths.

Altissimo ('DELmur')

■ *Climber, medium red, 1966, Delbard-Chabert*
These gorgeous single-petaled blooms (5 to 7 petals) are Chinese-lacquer red with bright yellow stamens. Flat and broad, the flowers look like large red saucers. The plant is vigorous, sending up lots of new canes throughout the year that bear large trusses of florets on very strong stems. Canes can reach a height of about 10 feet. Foliage is dark green. Scent is light. A spiral arrangement of the canes will improve bloom quantity. Zones 5 through 10.

Dream Weaver ('JACpicl')

■ *Climbing floribunda, orange pink, 1998, Zary*
Adapts well to training on pillars. For best effect train canes in a spiral formation around the structure. Flowers in small clusters are bright coral-pink with a slight old-rose scent. Long-lasting blooms have a rosette form (about 30 petals). Repeat bloom is relatively fast, and the plant is rarely without color. Foliage is dark green and glossy. Canes can grow 10 to 12 feet long, yielding a pillar height of about 8 feet. Zones 5 through 10.

'Paul's Lemon Pillar'
■ *Climbing hybrid tea, light yellow, 1915, Paul*
Elegant creamy white buds open to reveal light yellow centers that quickly turn almost white. The large flowers are cabbage-like, with broad overlapping petals. The flowers have a pronounced lemony fragrance. Blooms cannot withstand rainy days. Zones 5 through 10.

Climbing Rainbow's End ('SAVaclena')
■ *Miniature, yellow blend, 1999, Saville*
This variety has it all—good color, dense foliage, and a wonderful growth habit. Small clusters of blooms (35 petals, unscented) are deep yellow with red edges. Flowers age gracefully from bright yellow and red to deeper reds. Foliage is dark green. More compact than other pillar roses. Suitable for training on pillar and against a wall or fence, too. Grows 8 feet tall. Zones 5 through 11.

Summer Wine ('KORizont')
■ *Climber, deep pink, 1985, Kordes*
Small clusters of big, single, coral-pink flowers (five petals) with red stamens and a light yellow eye appear all summer. Fragrance will permeate the entire garden. An excellent cut flower. Vigorous plants grow 12 feet tall with glossy dark green foliage. Ideal for training on pillar, arbor, or pergola. Zones 5 through 10.

MORE EASY ROSES FOR PILLARS

Flutterbye ('WEKplasol')
■ *Floribunda, yellow blend, 1999, Carruth*
Large clusters of single-petaled blossoms carry different colors at the same time (yellow, coral, tangerine, and pink). 6 to 8 feet. Zones 5–9.

High Hopes ('HARyup')
■ *Climber, medium pink, 1994, Harkness*
Double pink blossoms (25 petals) in small clusters; strawberry fragrance. 10 to 12 feet. Zones 5–10. (Photo page 62.)

Paprika ('MEIriental')
■ *Climber, orange-red, 1997, Meilland*
Semidouble flowers (20 to 25 petals) are bright orange-red and have a light fragrance. Dense foliage is dark green. 8 to 10 feet. Zones 5–10. (Photo page 7.)

Pearly Gates ('WEKmeyer')
■ *Climber, medium pink, 1999, Meyer*
Angelic pink blooms with spicy-sweet fragrance. 8 to 12 feet. Zones 5–10. (Photo page 65.)

'Piñata'
■ *Climber, yellow blend, 1978, Suzuki*
Bright yellow flowers (25 to 30 petals) edged in fiery orange-red with strong, fruity aroma. 6 to 10 feet. Zones 6–10.

'William Baffin'
■ *Hybrid kordesii, deep pink, 1983, Svedja*
Spectacular parade of bawdy pink blooms (20 to 30 petals) in small clusters. Very winter-hardy. 10 to 12 feet. Zones 2–9. (Photos pages 7, 22.)

Eden Climber, Pierre de Ronsard ('MEIviolin')
■ *Climber, pink blend, 1987, Meilland*
Large, old-fashioned cupped flowers (40+ petals) in blend of pastel pink, cream, and yellow. Abundant blooms, one to a stem or in small clusters. Dark green foliage is dense clear to the ground. Vigorous plant grows up to 12 feet tall, lovely on a lamppost or gazebo. Zones 5 through 10.

Easiest Climbers for Arbors and Pergolas

Envelop yourself in flowers by growing a climber on an arch, arbor, or pergola. Each of these freestanding structures adds vertical interest to your garden. Even the smallest area can accommodate an arch, but arbors, and especially pergolas, need more space. Each has a different function. An arch is a narrow, curved span of wood or wrought iron through which you can walk; an arbor is a bower or shelter supporting climbing plants. A pergola is bigger and longer, consisting of parallel colonnades or uprights supporting an open roof of crossbeams. A pergola's uprights can be made of any strong material—stone, concrete, brick, or rot-resistant wood. Whatever the support it must be strong, because it has to support the substantial weight of the flowering canes.

The best roses to grow on these structures flower from ground level to the tips of their long canes. They bloom equally well on vertical and horizontal planes and produce canes at least 12 to 15 feet long, so that two plants can overlap and intertwine at the midpoint of the arch or pergola. Choose a self-cleaning rose that doesn't require constant grooming. Look for fragrant climbers to heighten your pleasure.

Flat-topped supports present a challenge for rose growers because many climbers have thick stems that easily break when forced to bend at a sharp angle. Ramblers, on the other hand, have slender stems and more flexibility; many, however, bloom only once each season. In these circumstances consider planting ramblers for the flat roof and climbers on the supporting walls. For optimal foliage density and flowers, plant roses 6 feet apart on both sides of a pergola.

High Hopes ('HARyup')
■ *Climber, medium pink, 1994, Harkness*

This is a true rose-pink color, rare among climbers. The buds are elegant, long, and pointed, opening to perfectly formed, high-centered blooms that exude the sweet scent of strawberries. Flowers are in small clusters on stems that are shorter than those of most climbers. Foliage is strong and healthy-looking but can suffer from a touch of black spot in humid climates. Spent blooms naturally fall away cleanly, initiating the next bloom cycle and keeping the bush tidy. Canes can grow 10 to 12 feet, ideal for training on an arbor, arch, pergola, or pillar. Zones 5 through 10.

'Sombreuil'
■ *Climbing tea, white, 1850, Robert*

This is one of the few teas roses that can cover a graceful arch, arbor, or pergola. White, frilly blooms often have creamy centers when first open that quickly turn to pure white, resembling old lace. Flowers are flat, quilled, quartered, and very double (almost 80 to 100 petals). The tea-rose fragrance is strong at first, then fades with age. An excellent variety to grow across an arch or arbor. Climbs 6 to 12 feet. Blooms continuously all summer. Zones 7 through 10.

Berries 'n' Cream ('POUlclimb')

■ *Climber, pink blend, 1999, Olesen*

Flowers are swirled with old-rose pink and creamy white, each floret differing from its neighbors. (In cool temperatures, more creamy white is visible.) Blooms (25 to 30 petals) are in bouquet-like clusters on strong, upright stems and are suitable for cutting. Canes can grow almost 10 to 12 feet—in mild climates, even larger—and have few thorns. Light green leaves are large and glossy. Zones 5 through 10.

Dublin Bay ('MACdub')

■ *Climber, medium red, 1975, McGredy*

Large, fully double, cardinal red flowers open in any climate—hot, cool, or mild. Slow to climb in first season but takes off in the next, achieving cane lengths of 10 feet. Flowers are in small clusters or sometimes one bloom to a stem. Excellent repeat flowering. Foliage is glossy, disease-resistant, and dark green. Zones 4 through 10.

MORE EASY ROSES FOR ARBORS AND PERGOLAS

'Aloha'

■ *Climbing hybrid tea, medium pink, 1949, Boerner*

Blooms are rose-pink with darker reverse, shapely and elegant with sweet rose fragrance. 6 to 10 feet. Zones 3–9.

America ('JACclam')

■ *Climber, orange-pink, 1976, Warriner, AARS*

Salmon-pink blooms (30 to 35 petals) have perfect form and rich dianthus perfume. 8 to 10 feet. Zones 4–10. (Photo page 6.)

'Golden Showers'

■ *Climber, medium yellow, 1956, Lammerts, AARS*

Masses of bright daffodil yellow flowers (25 to 30 petals) with sweet fragrance, bloom continuously all season. 10 to 12 feet. Zones 6–10.

'Mlle Cecile Brunner, Climbing'

■ *Climbing polyantha, light pink, 1894*

Large airy clusters of small, pointed, eggshell white buds open to silvery pink blooms with a spicy, sweet fragrance. Canes can grow to 20 feet to scramble over a wall, garden shed, or pergola. Zones 6–9.

Pearly Gates ('WEKmeyer')

■ *Climber, medium pink, 1999, Meyer*

Large pure pink blooms. Perfect form and sweet fragrance. Plants are vigorous and hardy. 8 to 12 feet. Zones 5–10. (Photo page 65.)

'Zephirine Drouhin'

■ *Bourbon, medium pink, 1868, Bizot*

Thornless variety that produces masses of fragrant cerise-pink blooms all season. 8 to 12 feet. Zones 5–8. (Photo page 11.)

'New Dawn'

■ *Climber, light pink, 1930, Van Fleet, WFRS*

Large, full, cameo pink flowers (40 to 45 petals), with sweet rose bouquet, appear all summer in small clusters (sometimes one bloom per stem). Canes can reach 12 to 20 feet. Foliage is glossy dark green and highly resistant to disease. Winter-hardy. Zones 4 through 10.

Easiest Climbers for High Walls

Ramblers and some climbers are ideal for covering large, vertical spaces. In warm climates ramblers (officially known as hybrid wichuraianas) can grow 30 to 50 feet in every direction if left untrained. This vigorous growth can cover large walls, houses, and trees with ease. Some climbers have canes more than 20 feet long, but their growth is upward and more restrained.

A wall or tree with roses adds drama to your garden, especially when the rose has masses of blooms. A wall of roses forms a colorful background for other plantings. Roses even bring life to an old tree, and their bloom time will not interfere with the tree's show of leaf color in fall.

Ramblers can grow as much as 25 feet in one season and form a gigantic mass within a few years. Although most small gardens cannot accommodate the breadth of an enormous plant, there may be room to use one rambler vertically on a tree or on the side of a house.

In a tree, a rambler weaves onto, over, and through the branches. Plant it as near as you can to the trunk. Spread the canes on the soil by the tree, then attach them to the trunk with twine or plastic landscape ties. Once the canes reach the branches, the rose supports itself. Remove dead canes and cut back protruding stems.

Similarly, you can plant a climber next to a large shrub and let the rose ramble up, over, and through it. This is a good idea for large, sturdy, early-spring- or fall-blooming shrubs, which may lack blossoms at the very time when the roses are in flower. The varieties recommended in this section need plenty of space and tend to be self-cleaning. They require little care.

Westerland ('KORwest')

■ *Shrub, apricot blend, 1969, Kordes*
Underappreciated for 30 years, this variety is now highly regarded for its blended, bright apricot-orange blooms (18 to 25 petals) with a strong spice and rose fragrance. Blooms have a ruffled look due to their serrated petals. Repeat blooming is fast. In mild climates canes reach 12 to 14 feet and will cover a house wall in only a few seasons. Zones 5 through 10.

Fourth of July ('WEKroalt')

■ *Climber, red blend, 1999, Carruth, AARS*
This vigorous new climber bears flowers (10 to 15 petals) all over the canes in large pleasing clusters. Each cluster is an explosion of velvety red striped with bright white and exuding a fresh-cut apple and sweet rose fragrance. Repeat bloom is very fast, and the bush appears to be in full color all summer. Foliage is sparkling green with excellent disease resistance. In mild climates canes can reach a length of 15 feet—enough to cover a wall, shed, or medium-sized tree. Also superb for an arbor or pergola. Zones 5 through 10.

MORE EASY ROSES FOR HIGH WALLS

'Dortmund'
■ *Hybrid kordesii, medium red, 1955, Kordes*
Large single-petaled flowers (five to seven petals) in small compact clusters with light scent. Needs regular removal of spent blooms to initiate next cycle. Excellent winter display of red hips. 8 to 10 feet. Zones 4–10. (Photo page 9.)

'Golden Showers'
■ *Climber, medium yellow, 1956, Lammerts, AARS*
Cheerful crops of sweet-scented yellow blooms appear all summer. Self-cleaning with good repeat. 10 to 12 feet. Zones 6–10.

'New Dawn'
■ *Climber, light pink, 1930, Van Fleet, WFRS*
Award-winning climber that boasts masses of fragrant cameo-pink flowers all summer. Canes can spread 12 to 20 feet. Zones 4–10. (Photo page 63.)

'Paul's Himalayan Musk Rambler'
■ *Hybrid musk, light pink, 1916, Paul*
Tree climber that sends out 30-foot stems in all directions. Fragrant drooping clusters of lilac-pink flowers appear as bountiful display once in spring. 12 to 20 feet. Zones 4–9.

Rosa banksiae lutea
■ *Species, light yellow, 1824*
Clusters of small, double, bright yellow flowers produced abundantly once in spring. Can grow up to 30 feet in all directions. Zones 7–10. (Photo page 9.)

'Zephirine Drouhin'
■ *Bourbon, medium pink, 1868, Bizot*
Thornless variety that produces masses of fragrant, cerise-pink blooms all season. 8 to 12 feet. Zones 5–8. (Photo page 11.)

Pearly Gates ('WEKmeyer')
■ *Climber, medium pink, 1999, Meyer*
Flowers (about 35 petals), exceptionally well-formed with symmetrical centers and sweet-spicy perfume, are pure pastel pink, shading to lighter tones toward outer petals as blossoms mature. Blooms all summer. Canes can reach 12 feet in a few seasons. Zones 5 through 10.

'Henry Kelsey'
■ *Hybrid kordesii, medium red, 1984, Svedja*

One of hardiest of all climbers. Clusters of semidouble dark red flowers (28 petals) highlighted with bright yellow stamens are produced all summer. Spicy fragrance. Plant has trailing and spreading habit 6 to 8 feet high, useful when trained as a climber or pillar. Needs little winter protection even in severe northern climates. Dense foliage is glossy green. Zones 3 through 9.

'Newport Fairy'
■ *Rambler, pink blend, 1908, Gardner*
This delightful hybrid wichuraiana bears enormous clusters of small, single-petaled, deep rose-pink blooms reminiscent of hydrangeas. The large sprawling bush reaches 20 to 30 feet in every direction. In mild climates canes develop into treelike trunks with vigor and can easily cover a hillside, house, or tree in a few years. Spring bloom is spectacular; repeat can be slow in cool climates. Zones 5 through 10.

The Easiest Roses for Small Spaces & Containers

Easiest Roses for Narrow Beds

A small garden changes the focus of rose growing from wide swaths of color to the beauty of individual plants. Even if crowded by plants, each rose stands alone when it comes to form and fragrance, because you see it up close. In small spaces use flowers of similar color intensity. Mixing strong and soft colors can be jarring.

In narrow beds and limited space, 8- to 12-foot trellised climbers work well on the walls of your house. Unless your house is very tall, ramblers would be too vigorous and hard to control for a small space.

Roses can work as foundation plantings in a small garden where you can plant a row of billowing miniatures, modern shrublets, or tall roses with a narrow upright habit. Make sure you plant the roses away from the drip line of the roof. Otherwise, the weight of snow in winter or sheets of water at other times of the year can damage tender canes and ruin the form of the plants. See that the eaves neither shade your roses nor block them from rain.

A circular island bed can have a big impact in a small garden. To create a dramatic focal point, develop a mound of flowers by layering plants of different heights. With the roses, plant a tall, narrow shrub in the middle, encircle it with shrublets, and edge it with miniatures. Remember to coordinate flowers of similar intensity. In this section you will find suitable varieties of small roses and recommendations for their uses.

Pillow Fight ('WEKpipogot')

■ *Shrub, white, 1999, Carruth*
Bright white flowers (about 35 petals) in large trusses. Fragrance is strong honey and rose scent. Glossy dark green foliage; strong upright stems. A "shrublet" that grows 2 to 3 feet tall. Ideal choice for mass planting in a border when spaced about 2 feet apart. Best in dry climates. Also good as container plant. Zones 4

Miss Flippins ('TUCkflip')
■ *Miniature, medium red, 1997, Tucker*

Well-formed red miniature with hybrid tea form blooms on small plant. Strong stems and glossy dark green foliage. Long-lasting, unscented flowers appear in large clusters in first flush of spring and in small sprays through summer. Minimal fading in hot weather. Also can be grown in container and as upright plant (2 to 3 feet tall) for accent in small spaces. Zones 5 through 11.

Rockin' Robin ('WEKboraco')
■ *Shrub, red blend, 1999, Carruth*

Profusion of red-, pink-, and white-striped 2-inch blooms (40 to 45 petals) in large clusters that last almost a month. Mild apple scent. Foliage is glossy green. Plant as low border or against wall in foundation bed. A shrublet that grows 2 to 3 feet tall in warm climates, shorter in cooler areas. Excellent for experimenting with color without devoting too much space to just one rose. Zones 4 through 9.

MORE EASY ROSES FOR NARROW BEDS

Baby Love ('SCRivluv')
■ *Miniature, deep yellow, 1992, Scrivens*

Blooms are bright yellow, colorfast, and single-petaled—a rare combination in miniatures. Outstanding resistance to black spot. 1 to 2 feet. Zones 4–11. (Photo page 47.)

Gizmo ('WEKcatlart')
■ *Miniature, orange blend, 1998, Carruth*

Perfectly mounded plant with abundant, single-petaled blooms, scarlet-orange with a white eye. 14 to 20 inches. Zones 5–10. (Photo page 20.)

Lemon Gems ('JACmiryl')
■ *Miniature, medium yellow, 1999, Walden, AOE*

Multipetaled flowers of rich deep yellow on a compact plant. 1 to 2 feet. Zones 5–10.

Petite Perfection ('JACrybi')
■ *Miniature, red blend, 1999, Walden*

Exquisite flowers of hybrid tea form, bright red with golden-yellow reverse. Stunning against glossy dark foliage. 2 to 3 feet. Zones 5–10.

Scentsational ('SAVamor')
■ *Miniature, mauve, 1995, Saville*

One of few miniatures with a powerful fragrance. Flowers have deep mauve edge in cool climates. 12 to 18 inches. Zones 5–11. (Photo page 46.)

What a Peach ('CHEwpeachdell')
■ *Shrub, apricot blend, 2002, Warner*

Warm apricot blooms in small clusters on tall upright plant. Moderately fruity fragrance. 2 to 3 feet. Zones 5–10. (Photo page 42.)

'Loving Touch'
■ *Miniature, apricot blend, 1983, Jolly, AOE*

Deep apricot buds mature into a lighter hue at the edges of the petals as the flowers open. The fragrant 1-inch blooms (25 petals) have a sculptured, symmetrical form with a texture like fine porcelain. They generally appear one to a stem and in small clusters. The foliage is attractive and disease-resistant. The bloom cycle is extremely fast and the bush is always in color. The flowers are superb for cutting. Plant about 2 feet apart for edging display. Bushes are well-rounded, 12 to 18 inches tall. Zones 5 through 10.

Jilly Jewel ('BENmfig')
■ *Miniature, medium pink, 2000, Benardella*

Elegant pure pink buds open slowly to flawless blooms (30 petals) in large clusters on strong upright stems. Blooms last at least a month. Disease-resistant foliage is attractive medium green. Bushes are strongly upright—1 to 2 feet tall—with little or no spreading. Plant 18 inches apart to achieve a dense edging. One plant by itself makes a stately, elegant, and colorful accent. Zones 5 through 11.

Easiest Roses for Containers

Roses grown in containers bring season-long color and fragrance to decks, patios, and balconies. Potted roses also work well as focal points in formal gardens, as border accents, in sunny doorways, and alongside garden gates and paths. Though many roses grow well in containers, the best choices are those that stay narrow and upright or form dense floral mounds. Upright roses are suited to a close grouping. Round bushes need more space; they look good standing alone or in more widely spread groups.

You can find containers made of terra-cotta, wood, or plastic (from plain to fancy) and as pots, tubs, urns, or planter boxes. Whatever you choose should work if it has the right shape and size. For miniatures use a 5- to 7-gallon container that's wider than it is deep. For floribundas and shrublets, choose a 10- to 12-gallon size. For hybrid teas and large shrubs, use a 20-gallon tub, urn, or box.

Soil composition is crucial when growing roses in a container. First, put a 2-inch layer of peat moss in the bottom of the container. Add a premium potting-soil mix around the plant's roots or root ball, stopping when the soil is 2 inches from the lip of the pot. Top with a 2-inch layer of bark mulch to preserve moisture during the hot summer months. A saucer under the container catches excess water and fertilizer. Fertilize roses regularly every two weeks; prevent buildup of salts by flushing the soil with water several times in succession every four weeks during dry weather. During rainy weather remove the saucer to allow the rain to do the leaching. In Zones 3 through 7 do not leave plants or containers outside over winter. Bury them or bring them into a cool, frost-free location such as an attached garage.

Ingrid Bergman ('POUlman')
■ *Hybrid tea, dark red, 1984, Olesen, WFRS*
World-class variety with powerfully fragrant velvety red flowers (35 petals), one to a stem. Color holds well without fading, even in hot climates. Blooms have exceptional form and are long-lasting, making them ideal as cut flowers. Repeat bloom is extremely rapid, with the next set of blooms forming before the current cycle has finished. Foliage is dark green, leathery, and disease-resistant. Habit is upright and tall, reaching 5 to 6 feet by the end of summer. Best planted in 20- to 25-gallon pot, tub, or half barrel. Zones 5 through 10 (Zones 8 through 10 in a container).

Glowing Amber ('MANglow')
■ *Miniature, red blend, 1996, Mander*
Scarlet-red 1-inch flowers with deep yellow undersides and golden stamens unfurl slowly. The blooms are double (26 to 40 petals), with flawless form. As they age the scarlet tones deepen and intensify. The plant grows 12 to 15 inches tall with a strongly upright compact habit. Exquisite in a 12- to 14-inch pot. Zones 5 through 10 (Zones 8 through 10 in a container).

Outta the Blue ('WEKstiphitsu')

■ *Shrub, mauve, 2002, Carruth*

A new-generation rose that captures the coveted look of antique roses. Flowers (25 to 30 petals—in big gorgeous clusters—are many-toned, with rich magenta to lavender-blue hues, spiked with yellow. Strong clove-and-rose fragrance. Plant is upright to slightly rounded, 3 to 4 feet tall. Best in a 20-gallon container. Zones 5 through 10 (Zones 8 through 10 in a container).

Minnie Pearl ('SAVahowdy')

■ *Miniature, pink blend, 1982, Saville*

Long regarded as standard of excellence for miniatures. Elegant buds open slowly into perfectly symmetrical, high-centered, light pink flowers (35 to 40 petals) with darker undersides. The 1-inch blooms are one to a stem or sometimes in clusters on strong straight stems. Plants are well-rounded, 12 to 24 inches tall. Repeat cycle is relatively fast (35 to 40 days). In intense heat, color may fade. Zones 5 through 10 (Zones 8 through 10 in a container).

French Lace ('JAClace')

■ *Floribunda, white, 1980, Warriner, AARS*

Elegant pastel apricot to creamy off-white blooms (30 to 35 petals) in small sprays. Large and well-formed blooms call to mind antique lace. Mild, fruity fragrance. Produces best colors in cool temperatures. Hardy in cold climates only with winter protection. Grows upright and compact, reaching 3 to 4 feet tall. Foliage is dark green and glossy. Best in a 15-gallon or larger container. Zones 6 through 10 (Zones 8 through 10 in a container).

MORE EASY ROSES FOR CONTAINERS

Behold ('SAVahold')

■ *Miniature, medium yellow, 1996, Saville*

Bright yellow flowers with lighter yellow reverse. 12 to 20 inches. Zones 5–11. (Photo page 34.)

Hot Tamale ('JACpoy')

■ *Miniature, yellow blend, 1993, Zary, AOE*

Glowing yellow-orange blooms in nonstop abundance on low-growing plant. 12 to 15 inches. Zones 5–11. (Photo page 46.)

Knock Out ('RADrazz')

■ *Shrub, red blend, 1999, Radler, AARS*

Completely disease-free plants loaded with light red to deep pink flowers in large clusters. 4 to 6 feet. Zones 4–10. (Photos pages 10, 20, 38.)

Little Flame ('JACnuye')

■ *Miniature, orange blend, 1998, Walden, AOE*

Big intense orange flowers last well and mature to rich burnt orange, then clean quickly with little need for deadheading. 1 to 2 feet. Zones 5–10.

'Party Girl'

■ *Miniature, yellow blend, 1979, Saville, AOE*

Immaculate, well-formed, apricot-yellow blooms in gigantic clusters (18 to 24 blooms per stem). Growth habit is well-rounded and low. 1 to 2 feet. Zones 5–11.

Petite Perfection ('JACrybi')

■ *Miniature, red blend, 1999, Walden*

Shapely, elegant, bright red blooms with golden-yellow reverse. Plants are upright. 2 to 3 feet. Zones 5–10.

Sexy Rexy ('MACrexy')

■ *Floribunda, medium pink, 1984, McGredy*

Upright plant produces huge trusses of flowers on strong stems all summer. 4 to 5 feet. Zones 5–11. (Photos pages 6, 79.)

Stainless Steel ('WEKblusi')

■ *Hybrid tea, mauve, 1991, Carruth*

Long tall stems show off elegant blooms (25 to 30 petals) of subtle coloration. Plant is upright. 6 to 8 feet. Zones 5–11.

Sun Flare ('JACjam')

■ *Floribunda, medium yellow, 1981, Warriner, AARS*

Perfect for patio. Growth habit is mounded. Light licorice fragrance. 3 to 4 feet. Zones 5–10. (Photos pages 7, 25, 49.)

World War II Memorial Rose ('WEZgrey')

■ *Hybrid tea, mauve, 2000, Weeks*

Smoky blooms are soft white with gray and tinge of lavender. Upright plant. 4 to 6 feet. Zones 5–10.

Easiest Roses for Hanging and Cascading Effects

Some rose varieties have a natural tendency to spread and drape, making them ideal behind a retaining wall. These varieties, with flexible canes drooping gracefully and flowering along the length of the cane, are also ideal for hanging baskets. Using roses in a hanging basket gives them the advantage of excellent air circulation, which helps prevent fungal disease. Roses in this category are limited to miniatures and some climbing varieties with fast repeat cycles that keep their colorful display throughout the growing season.

One effective way to make a hanging basket is to use a container that is much wider than it is deep. This permits the plant to generate a strong root system, because the roots are protected from heat damage. The wide container also provides an ideal platform to support the canes before they start drooping over the edge. Because a hanging basket is suspended and exposed, it needs a 1- to 2-inch lining of peat moss as a protective barrier against moisture loss on hot days. And because plants receive some shade on most patios, the varieties recommended here are tolerant of less than the required six to eight hours of sunshine per day. Hanging baskets need to be watered more frequently than plants in the ground, and the soil mix should never be allowed to dry out. Plastic self-watering hanging pots that incorporate a sizable water-holding chamber are an excellent choice to minimize your watering chores.

Sweet Chariot ('MORchari')
■ *Miniature, mauve, 1984, Moore*
Deep lavender to royal purple flowers mature to lavender hues, lasting for weeks. Blooms have the look and feel of old garden roses (about 40 petals) and come in large clusters with a delicious, heavy damask perfume. Canes arch naturally downward, perfect for a hanging basket. Within a season canes will completely cover a 5- to 7-gallon container. Zones 5 through 10.

'Green Ice'
■ *Miniature, white, 1971, Moore*
Tiny white buds open slowly to reveal soft white to green flowers. Large trusses usually start off with a hint of pink, then acquire a light green hue. Glossy bright green foliage. Plant is wide and spreading, and its canes bend or arch under weight of their heavy floral sprays. Relatively small plants, they need a 3- to 4-gallon container. 2 to 3 feet. Zones 5 through 11.

MORE EASY ROSES FOR HANGING AND CASCADING

Chick-a-Dee, Climbing ('MORclchick')

■ *Climbing miniature, medium pink, 2000, Moore*

Ideal cascading plant with soft pink flowers. Canes can grow 3 to 4 feet long. Zones 5–10.

Gourmet Popcorn ('WEOpop')

■ *Miniature, white, 1986, Desamero*

Ideal hanging basket plant with both upright and spreading growth, and massive trusses of pristine white blooms. 2 to 3 feet. Zones 4–10. (Photos pages 9, 34.)

'Renae'

■ *Climbing floribunda, medium pink, 1954, Moore*

Floriferous small climber with canes that bend to the ground. 4 to 6 feet. Zones 5–9.

Renny ('MOReny')

■ *Miniature, medium pink, 1989, Moore*

Profuse pink flowers with old-fashioned fragrance and form. Thornless canes. 3 to 4 feet. Zones 5–11.

'Orange Honey'

■ *Miniature, orange blend, 1979, Moore*

Pointed buds open to luscious yellow-amber petals that unfurl to cupped, pure orange-yellow flowers (23 petals). Blossoms develop reddish color late in season. Fragrance is fruity. Prolific flower production, spreading plant habit. When the rose is grown in partial shade, bright orange flowers can last for weeks. Best in 4-gallon pot. 2 to 3 feet. Zones 5 through 11.

Sequoia Gold ('MORsegold')

■ *Miniature, medium yellow, 1986, Moore, AOE*

Bright cheery yellow flowers mature to pale scintillating yellow. The 1-inch florets are double (30 petals) with decidedly fruity fragrance. Stems, bearing small clusters of three to seven flowers, grow upright, then arch. Fast bloom repeat for color all summer. A creation from the father of miniature roses, Ralph Moore. 1 to 2 feet. Zones 5 through 11.

'Red Cascade'

■ *Climbing miniature, dark red, 1976, Moore, AOE*

Perhaps the first climber adapted for hanging baskets, with long cascading canes that reach several feet over the edge of the container. The deep red 1-inch flowers (40 petals) have a light fragrance. Small leathery leaves. Plant needs full sun all day and good air circulation. Canes can droop to the ground with flowers along their entire length. Bloom repeat is relatively fast. 3 to 4 feet. Zones 5 through 11.

Easiest Small Climbers for Vertical Effects

Some small climbers, shrubs, and miniatures provide height and dense coverage, with flowers and foliage along the length of their stems for a full, lush appearance. Moreover, varieties that grow only 3 to 5 feet tall look groomed and require little maintenance to control their width and height. Short climbers provide a blaze of color in an upright growth pattern without invading nearby plants. This tidy behavior makes them ideal for small spaces. With grooming some ground-cover roses can also be trained to grow vertically in a small area.

In containers small climbers can expand the intimate landscape of a deck, patio, or balcony into the vertical dimension. Cultivate them in decorative 15- to 20-gallon pots and tubs, and provide a simple lattice to support the canes. The lattice should be rectangular and about 3 to 4 feet wide, or fan-shaped and about 5 feet wide at the top. As the plant grows weave the canes neatly into the lattice to ensure complete coverage of the support and create a wall of living color on your patio or deck. If you like, you can plant other blooming plants around the base for seasonal displays of flowers.

Earthquake, Climbing ('MORshook')
■ *Climbing miniature, red blend, Moore, 1990*
Double flowers (40 petals) are striped bright red and yellow, with yellow reverse, in small clusters of 3 to 5 florets that cover the plant. Color contrasts and depth of color are best in cool climates, where striped aspect is more pronounced. Spectacular against a wall or a fence. After the first bloom flush the repeat bloom is somewhat reduced but still dazzling. Grows 4 to 6 feet tall. Zones 6 through 10.

'Lavender Lassie'
■ *Hybrid musk, mauve, 1960, Kordes*
This shrub can be successfully trained as a young plant to climb on a lattice. Blooms appear on long stems that arch slightly under the weight of clusters. Flowers are pleasing rose-pink with a hint of lavender. Blooms are rosettes (60+ petals) with noticeable fragrance. 6 to 8 feet. Zones 4 through 9.

Work of Art ('MORart')
■ *Climbing miniature, orange blend, 1989, Moore*

Short buds open to elegant, urn-shaped orange blooms with undersides that are blended with yellow. Blooms are double (35 petals), held in small tight clusters on strong stems. Flowers are long-lasting, maturing to a range of orange hues. Vigorous; in warm climates it will reach 4 to 6 feet in the first season. Canes perform best if fanned out to a width of 4 to 5 feet. Best in a 15-gallon container. Zones 5 through 10.

MORE EASY SMALL CLIMBERS FOR VERTICAL EFFECTS

Cal Poly, Climbing ('MORclpoly')
■ *Climbing miniature, medium yellow, 1997, Moore*
Just like its bush counterpart, this plant has bright yellow flowers (20 petals) and handsome foliage. 4 to 6 feet. Zones 5–11.

Chick-a-dee, Climbing ('MORclchick')
■ *Climbing miniature, medium pink, 2000, Moore*
Double pink blossoms in profusion on this climbing descendant of the bush counterpart. 3 to 4 feet. Zones 5–10.

Cliffs of Dover ('POUlemb')
■ *Shrub, white, 1996, Olesen*
White single-petaled blooms with yellow centers all summer. Excellent disease resistance. Zones 4–10. (Photo page 11).

'Lavender Lace, Climbing'
■ *Climbing miniature, mauve, 1971, Rumsey*
Pure lavender blooms open fast to reveal large golden stamens. 4 to 6 feet. Zones 5–11.

'Jeanne LaJoie'
■ *Climbing miniature, medium pink, 1975, Sima, AOE*

Nonstop bloom production starts with long pointed buds that open to nonfading medium pink flowers (35 to 40 petals) of exquisite hybrid tea form, with a hint of fragrance. Dark green leaves are small, glossy, and embossed. Strong sturdy canes (6 to 10 feet long) can easily be trained into horizontal positions to promote maximum bloom. Plant 4 feet apart. Zones 4 through 11.

'Candy Cane'
■ *Climbing miniature, pink blend, 1958, Moore*

Classic miniature climber of long-standing popularity with dashing semidouble blooms (13 to 15 petals) that are striped deep pink and pure white. Massive clusters with up to 20 blooms often arch on canes to form candy-cane shape (hence its name). Sprays can last for weeks. Remove spent blooms to improve repeat bloom cycle. Grows 4 to 6 feet tall, depending on climate, and is ideal against a wall. Easy to grow and maintain. Training is simple on supports because canes are pliable. In humid climates black spot can be a problem. Zones 5 through 11.

Easiest Roses for Standards and Patio Trees

Tree roses, or standards, are rosebushes raised several feet off the ground by grafting them onto rose stock grown to several feet tall. Because the flowers are elevated, the form and color of the bush are easy to see. Tree roses have the top-heavy look of topiary. They make excellent focal points and can dominate the center of a bed or bring height and color to a border. They can flank a gate, a piece of sculpture, or the entrance to a path. They make their adjoining structure look important, framing it with color and whimsical form.

The best tree roses come from varieties with well-rounded shapes. Standards look best when they bloom all over the crown rather than point up to the sky like a typical hybrid tea. Floribundas, polyanthas, miniatures, and mini-floras all make attractive tree roses, some of which have a weeping effect.

Even for normally hardy rose varieties, the graft union of a tree rose is highly vulnerable to freezing and dessication in winter. In mild-winter climates, growing tree roses in the ground adds a new dimension to your garden. North of Zone 8, however, it's best to grow tree roses in containers. Water the pots well before bringing them indoors in fall, and set them in a basement or attached garage where temperatures remain cool without freezing— and where the roses will remain dormant over the winter. In spring, move the containers outdoors. The USDA Hardiness Zones provided for the roses below are for nonstandard plants grown in the ground.

You can buy standards as 36-inch trees, 24-inch trees (known as patio trees), 18-inch trees (suited for miniature roses), and in some cases, 60- or 72-inch spilling or weeping trees. Short tree roses need no permanent support, though a support rod is advisable for the first few years. You may need an umbrella-shaped support for large, weeping trees.

Weeping China Doll

◼ *Polyantha, medium pink, 1977, Weeks*
The all-time favorite weeping tree rose (60-inch standard). Long thornless canes arch gracefully downward, covered with large trusses of small cupped flowers of rose-pink with a base of chrome-yellow (20 to 25 petals). Slight tea scent. Foliage is narrow, leathery, and apple green. Repeat flowering is excellent without any care. After a few seasons the canopy will be large and imposing, requiring some support to train and guide canes into correct positions. Best in 15- to 20-gallon container. Zones 5 through 10.

Purple Heart ('WEKbipuhit')
◼ *Floribunda, mauve, 1999, Carruth*
A modern rose with an old-fashioned look. The cupped, deep wine red blooms (30 to 35 petals) have a strong, spicy-clove perfume. Flowers are larger in cool climates. Foliage is matte green. Bloom repeat is good to moderate. Tends to weep if canes are not cut back to promote side growth. Available as 24- and 36-inch trees. Best in 15- to 20-gallon container. Zones 5 through 10.

MORE EASY ROSES FOR STANDARDS AND PATIO TREES

60-INCH WEEPING OR CASCADING TREES
Plant in a 20-gallon container.

Flower Girl ('FRYyeoman')
■ *Shrub, light pink, 1999, Fryer*
Huge soft pink trusses loaded with blossoms (8 to 15 petals). Grows more like a hydrangea than a rose. Zones 7–9.

Pillow Fight ('WEKpipogop')
■ *Shrub, white, 1999, Carruth*
Bright white blooms (about 35 petals) in large tight sprays. Zones 7–9. (Photos pages 9, 66.)

'The Fairy'
■ *Polyantha, light pink, 1932, Bentall*
Small soft pink flowers with mild apple fragrance in large pyramidal clusters that bend gracefully to the ground. Glossy green foliage. Zones 7–10. (Photo page 21.)

36-INCH STANDARDS
Plant in 10- to 15-gallon container.

'Angel Face'
■ *Floribunda, mauve, 1968, Swim & Weeks, AARS*
Ruffled fragrant lavender blooms (25 to 30 petals) with strong citrus scent. Small clusters cover entire bush. Zones 8–10.

Iceberg ('KORbin')
■ *Floribunda, white, 1958, Kordes*
Looks even better as tree than bush. 3 to 4 feet. Zones 8–10. (Photos pages 9, 32.)

Veteran's Honor ('JACopper')
■ *Hybrid tea, dark red, 1999, Zary*
Elegant dark red blooms (25 to 30 petals) on long stems suitable for cutting. Zones 8–10. (Photo page 30.)

18- AND 24-INCH PATIO TREES
Plant in a 5- to 7-gallon container.

Hot Tamale ('JACpoy')
■ *Miniature, yellow blend, 1993, Zary, AOE*
Glowing yellow-orange blooms. Zones 8–11. (Photo page 46.)

Lemon Gems ('JACmiryl')
■ *Miniature, medium yellow, 1999, Walden, AOE*
Profusion of colorfast blossoms in rich deep yellow. Zones 8–10.

Rainbow's End ('SAValife')
■ *Miniature, yellow blend, 1984, Saville, AOE*
Yellow blooms edged in red mature to all red. Zones 8–11. (Photos pages 11, 35.)

exude a powerful rose fragrance. Flower stems drape elegantly toward the ground, making this rose ideal as a 24-inch patio tree or in a hanging basket. Small leaves are deep green with good disease resistance. Best in 15- to 20-gallon container. Zones 5 through 10.

Brilliant Pink Iceberg ('PRObril')
■ *Floribunda, pink blend, 1999, Weatherly*
All the popular characteristics of its parent, Iceberg, but with a striking new flower color: bright cerise-pink painted onto cream. Flowers (18 to 24 petals) are in showy clusters with mild honey scent and lasting quality, even in hot climates. Color is more intense in cool climates. Available as a 36-inch standard or 24-inch patio tree. Best in a 15- to 20-gallon container. Zones 5 through 10.

Sweet Chariot ('MORchari')
■ *Miniature, mauve, 1984, Moore*
Fluffy flowers (40 to 50 petals) are magenta, purple, and lavender, creating a spectrum of color as they age. In moderate temperatures the lavender hues are more intense. Trusses

Baby Grand ('POUlit')
■ *Miniature, medium pink, 1994, Poulsen*
Makes a perfect 18-inch standard. Flowers (30 to 35 petals) are pure pink with the quartered form of an old garden rose. Slight apple scent. Plant has neat, compact round habit only 12 to 16 inches tall. Sprays are long-lasting and repeat bloom is rapid. Ideal for small patio in ornate, Italian-style pot. Best in a 5- to 10-gallon container. Zones 5 through 10.

The Easiest Roses for Cut Flowers & Fragrance

Easiest Roses for Long-Stemmed Cutting

Because of their sometimes leggy habit, hybrid teas may not be the prettiest shrubs in the garden, but you can't beat their flowers for cutting. Their long, sturdy stems, elegant buds, and long-lasting blooms make them perfect for bouquets and flower arranging. When choosing hybrid teas look for many-petaled flowers because they take longer to open than blooms with fewer petals and thus last longer in the vase.

To ensure bigger blooms and longer stems, cut off the small buds beside the central bud as soon as they start to develop. These smaller buds take energy from the main bloom.

Long-stemmed roses are easy to arrange, whether you want one rosebud in a narrow vase or a bouquet with baby's breath in a larger container. If you intend to set your arrangement on a side table against a wall, consider a symmetrical design in a flat fan-shaped vase. Arrange the flowers to form an arc from the center down either side. Hold the stems in place with glass marbles, or buy a special vase with separate holes for each stem to keep the blooms from touching and blurring individual shapes.

Traditional rose bowls—usually 4 to 6 inches high—make perfect centerpieces for dinner parties. Set a wire grid on top of the bowl to keep the roses in place, or use floral foam, which retains moisture and stabilizes the arrangement.

The varieties listed here make good cut flowers because they naturally grow one to a stem—in profusion—and repeat fairly fast. Blooms are always on long stems, are complemented by attractive foliage, and have sufficient stamina to survive indoors for five to seven days after you cut them.

Kardinal ('KORlingo')

■ *Hybrid tea, medium red, 1986, Kordes*

This classic variety is often preferred by professional arrangers for its holding capacity. Elegant long stems support shapely buds opening to almost porcelain-looking creations that last remarkably long when cut. Fragrance is light. Foliage is dark green. Plant grows 4 to 6 feet tall and repeats well in most climates. Zones 5 through 10.

Elina ('DICjana')

■ *Hybrid tea, light yellow, 1984, Dickson*

White buds open to elegant, large, light yellow flowers (35+ petals) with deeper cream centers. Fragrance is light. Bush is vigorous and disease-resistant, with dense, glossy dark green foliage. It can grow 6 to 8 feet tall in moderate climates. Zones 5 through 10.

MORE EASY ROSES FOR LONG-STEMMED CUTTING

Barbra Streisand ('WEKquaneze')
■ *Hybrid tea, mauve, 1999, Carruth*
Large clusters of well-formed blooms in deep lavender blushed with purple. Fantastic old garden rose fragrance. 3 to 6 feet. Zones 5–10. (Photo page 30.)

Bride's Dream ('KORoyness')
■ *Hybrid tea, light pink, 1985, Kordes*
Long, elegant, angelic pastel pink blooms (30 to 35 petals) with porcelain look. Can grow to 6 to 8 feet. Zones 5–10. (Photo page 6.)

Crystalline ('ARObipy')
■ *Hybrid tea, white, 1987, Christensen & Carruth*
Weatherproof snowy white flowers have almost 35 petals and open slowly. Sweet tea fragrance. 5 to 6 feet. Zones 5–10. (Photo page 24.)

Jardins de Bagatelle ('MEImafris')
■ *Hybrid tea, white, 1986, Meilland*
Perfectly formed creamy pink flowers tipped with pale pink, mainly one to a stem. Strong rose bouquet. 4 to 6 feet. Zones 5–9.

Moonstone ('WEKcryland')
■ *Hybrid tea, white, 1998, Carruth*
Huge, pure, bright white flowers finely edged with delicate pink. 5 to 7 feet. Zones 5–10. (Photo page 31.)

New Zealand ('MACgenev')
■ *Hybrid tea, light pink, 1989, McGredy*
Soft creamy pink blooms. Stunning fragrance. Long stems. 4 to 6 feet. Zones 5–10. (Photo page 20.)

Peter Mayle ('MEIzincaro')
■ *Hybrid, deep pink, 2001, Meilland*
Large blooms (4 to 5 inches across) have heavy, old garden rose perfume. 4 to 6 feet. Zones 5–10. (Photo page 55.)

Toulouse Lautrec ('MEIrevolt')
■ *Hybrid tea, medium yellow, 1994, Meilland*
Solid lemon-colored flowers with old-fashioned look. Strong lemon scent. 4 to 6 feet. Zones 5–9. (Photo page 7.)

Veteran's Honor ('JACopper')
■ *Hybrid tea, dark red, 1999, Zary*
Has set a new standard for dark red roses. Thick petal substance makes blooms ideal for cutting. 5 to 7 feet. Zones 5–10. (Photo page 30.)

Love & Peace ('BALpeace')
■ *Hybrid tea, yellow blend, 2002, Lim & Twomey, AARS*
Large symmetrical blooms (40+ petals) are yellow with deep pink to red blush. Mild fragrance. Best flower production is in humid climates. Color is most intense in moderate climates. Medium disease resistance. Grows 5 to 6 feet high. Zones 5 through 10.

'Royal Highness'
■ *Hybrid tea, light pink, 1962, Swim & Weeks, AARS*
Large, high-centered, pale pink blooms (43+ petals) with a porcelain texture are exceptionally well-formed and symmetrical. Borne singly on long straight stems, the strongly fragrant blooms (sweet tea fragrance) open slowly. Rarely forms clusters. Repeat bloom is relatively fast in moderate climates. Bloom size and color are best in moderate temperatures. Plants are vigorous, upright, and bushy (5 to 7 feet tall). Lustrous foliage is bright green and exceptionally disease-resistant. Zones 5 through 10.

Valencia ('KOReklia')
■ *Hybrid tea, apricot blend, 1989, Kordes*
Huge, full, high-centered flowers (30 to 40 petals) are pure copper-yellow without any shading or blemish. Highly symmetrical. Sweet and enduring fragrance. Plant reaches 5 to 6 feet tall and can be somewhat angular in shape, making it more appropriate for the cutting garden than a bed or hedge. Large leathery leaves are deep green. Zones 5 through 10.

Easiest Clustered Roses for Bouquets-on-a-Stem

You don't need long-stemmed roses for a lovely bouquet. In fact, just about any kind of rose is a good addition to a flower arrangement. Grandiflora roses bear flower clusters with the classic look of hybrid teas; floribundas produce immense sprays of lovely blooms. For cutting purposes buy plants with lavish sprays and strong stems capable of supporting weighty clusters.

To extend the life of your arrangement and encourage further blooms, follow these suggestions for cutting. The best time of day to cut roses is early morning (when the air is cool) or early evening (when flowers have stored up food from the day). Start cutting when roses are in bud. If it's a long-stemmed hybrid tea rose, you can tell the bud is ready to be cut when its sepals separate and curl down. If the flower has begun to bloom, cut it when it's one-third to one-half open. If you're cutting cluster-flowered roses, make sure that the main bloom of the cluster is open and the rest are in various phases of bud. Snip off the open flower to encourage more buds to

bloom. Cut stems at a 45-degree angle and above a leaf bud to promote more flowering.

Bring along a bucket of water whenever you cut roses so that you can immerse the stems immediately after you snip them. Once indoors, cut the stems again—this time under water—and leave them in the bucket. Set the bucket in a cool, dimly lit spot for at least two hours, and preferably overnight, to condition the blooms. Before arranging the flowers clean their container thoroughly. Fill it with water, adding some lemon-lime soda (regular, not diet) or floral preservative to lengthen the life of the blooms. Snip off leaves and thorns below the water line.

Varieties chosen here satisfy four essential requirements. First, the spray structure is upright, with all flowers at nearly the same level. Second, stems contain flowers at all stages of development, ensuring a longer lifetime. Third, cut stems survive at least seven to 10 days in the home. Finally, the variety is capable of producing strong straight stems continuously and vigorously.

Gold Medal ('AROyqueli')
■ *Grandiflora, medium yellow, 1982, Christensen*
Deep yellow blooms (30+ petals) with burnt orange to red edge in open trusses. Flowers have long vase life. Vigorous tall (5 to 7 feet) upright bush. Leaf cutter bee often makes telltale half-moon cutouts on leaves. Zones 5 through 10.

'Duet'
■ *Hybrid tea, medium pink, 1960, Swim, AARS*
This classic hybrid tea should have been classified as a grandiflora because it sends up tight clusters of blooms rather than one bloom per stem. Flowers are large (4 inches across) and continually produced in vast quantities. Blooms (30+ petals) are light pink, with deep pink on the reverse. Clusters have good bloom repeat. Plant grows 6 to 8 feet tall with upright habit. Zones 5 through 11.

Sexy Rexy ('MACrexy')

■ *Floribunda, medium pink, 1984, McGredy*
Upright stems carry massive clusters of 20 or more blooms (40 petals) that look like camellias when fully opened. Blooms fade a little at edges upon maturing but last for weeks. Pleasant fragrance. Repeat bloom is good but requires removal of spent flowers to encourage next cycle. Small leaves are overpowered by large flower clusters. 4 to 5 feet tall. Zones 5 through 11.

MORE EASY ROSES FOR BOUQUETS-ON-A-STEM

Berries 'n' Cream ('POUlclimb')

■ *Climber, pink blend, 1999, Olesen*
Old-rose pink and creamy white sprays like a floribunda. 10 to 12 feet. Zones 5–10. (Photo page 63.)

Brilliant Pink Iceberg ('PRObril')

■ *Floribunda, pink blend, 1999, Weatherly*
Big splash of cerise-pink blended with creamy white. 3 to 4 feet. Zones 5–10. (Photos pages 7, 75.)

Easy Going ('HARflow')

■ *Floribunda, yellow blend, 1999, Harkness*
Golden peachy yellow blooms. Lovely glossy green foliage. 3 to 4 feet. Zones 5–10.

Fabulous ('JACrex')

■ *Floribunda, white, 2000, Zary*
Sparkling blossoms (25 to 30 petals) in exceptionally large clusters with light fragrance. 4 to 5 feet. Zones 5–10.

Fragrant Apricot ('JACgrant')

■ *Floribunda, apricot blend, 1998, Zary*
Copper-tinted blooms (30 petals) deepen to dusty pink. Strong musk fragrance. 4 to 5 feet. Zones 5–10.

Lavaglut ('KORlech')

■ *Floribunda, dark red, 1978, Kordes*
Massive clusters of long-lasting, intensely deep red blooms (25 petals) with velvety texture. 3 to 5 feet. Zones 5–10. (Photo page 33.)

Love Potion ('JACsedi')

■ *Floribunda, mauve, 1993, Christensen*
Deep purple blooms (20 to 25 petals) in clusters against shiny dark green foliage. Raspberry scent. 4 to 5 feet. Zones 5–10.

Showbiz ('TANweieke')

■ *Floribunda, medium red, 1983, Tantau, AARS*
Brilliant fire engine red blooms (25 petals) in great clusters, sometimes as many as 30 blooms per stem. 3 to 4 feet. Zones 5–10. (Photo page 6.)

Brass Band ('JACcofl')

■ *Floribunda, apricot blend, 1993, Christensen, AARS*
Large clusters of double blooms (30 to 35 petals) in a dazzling blend of melon, papaya, and apricot appear all summer and can last for weeks when cut. Fruity fragrance. In cool climates colors may be deeper. 4 to 5 feet tall. Zones 5 through 10.

Blueberry Hill ('WEKcryplag')

■ *Floribunda, mauve, 1999, Carruth*
Colorfast flowers (12 to 25 petals) with bright golden stamens in small tight upright clusters. Blooms smell like freshly baked apple pie. Foliage is clean, glossy, dark green. Sprays can be tightly packed in vase. Plant habit is rounded, 3 to 4 feet tall. Zones 5 through 10.

Easiest Roses for Old-Fashioned Bouquets

Old-fashioned roses make glorious flower arrangements. Throughout history artists have chosen to paint them for their poignant, sensual beauty. Their colors—from pure white to shades of pink, deep purple, and dark red—harmonize when they are grouped informally together in a vase. Their forms can be pure and single or lush with petals and leaves. Their fragrance can be nearly overwhelming, a powerful, sweet scent that wafts through several rooms of the house.

Full old-rose blossoms with many petals rest heavily on their stems and droop gracefully over the edge of a vase. Unlike long-stemmed hybrid teas, old-rose stems are short and flexible and often bear small sprays of flowers. Many bloom just once a year in late spring or early summer. Contemporary English roses and many other modern repeat-blooming shrubs emulate the form and fragrance of old-fashioned flowers while retaining the vigor and longer stems of shrubs.

If your arrangement includes both modern shrub roses and old-fashioned roses, place those with stronger stems in the middle and use the shorter stems toward the edges. Choose blooms in bud or slightly open, because old roses quickly shed their petals once fully open. For modern shrubs with stronger, straighter stems, arranging is easier. Set floral foam in a low bowl and insert the rose stems and a few wild ferns from the yard for a glorious bouquet.

NOSEGAYS

Make an old-fashioned nosegay for a friend. Pick a rose for the center. Surround it with herbs and flowers such as pinks, thyme, and lavender until it measures 4 inches wide. Frame the bouquet with leaves of sage, anise hyssop, or scented geranium. Tie the stems together and trim them to 4 inches. Insert the stems into a tiny vase, or make a handle by covering them with damp paper towels topped with a layer of plastic wrap. At this point you can insert the handle into a paper doily or a circle of lace with a hole cut from the middle. Wrap the handle with florist's tape and tie a bow with streamers around the base of the bouquet.

days before shattering. Plant climbs 6 to 12 feet. Zones 7 through 10.

'Paul Neyron'
■ *Hybrid perpetual, medium pink, 1869, Levet*
Massive, flat, pure pink to rose-pink flowers on strong, straight stems suitable for the center of a romantic bouquet. The cupped flowers have more than 50 petals and resemble peonies. Flowers last weeks. Fragrance is moderate. Plant habit is vigorous, tall (4 to 5 feet), and upright. Large leaves are rich medium green. Zones 5 through 10.

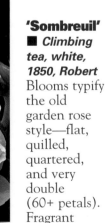

'Sombreuil'
■ *Climbing tea, white, 1850, Robert*
Blooms typify the old garden rose style—flat, quilled, quartered, and very double (60+ petals). Fragrant flowers in small- to medium-sized compact sprays have creamy white centers that quickly turn to sparkling white. Blooms cut at half-open stage last indoors at least a week. At the fully-opened stage blooms last only a few

MORE EASY ROSES FOR OLD-FASHIONED BOUQUETS

Belle Story ('AUSelle')
■ *Shrub, light pink, 1985, Austin*
Large cupped flowers with contrasting yellow stamens. Plant 30 inches apart for mass display. 4 to 6 feet. Zones 5–9.

'Celine Forestier'
■ *Noisette, light yellow, 1858, Leroy*
Quartered pale yellow blooms with dark green button at center; spicy fragrance. 5 to 6 feet. Zones 7–10.

'Great Maiden's Blush'
■ *Alba, white, before 1738*
Fragrant blush pink flowers on a large arching shrub with grayish foliage. 4 to 6 feet. Zones 3–9.

'Henri Martin'
■ *Moss, medium red, 1862, Laffay*
Claret red to crimson blooms in large clusters open flat on large shrub. 5 to 6 feet. Zones 3–9.

'Henry Hudson'
■ *Hybrid rugosa, white, 1976, Svejda*
Double flowers with a hint of pink at petal tips; good fragrance. 3 to 4 feet. Zones 3–9.

'Marchesa Boccella' (Jacques Cartier)
■ *Hybrid perpetual, light pink, 1842, Desprez*
Large double quartered blooms on upright plant. Fragrant. 3 to 4 feet. Zones 4–10.

'Mme Hardy'
■ *Damask, white, 1832, Hardy*
One of most beautiful whites, with attractive green pip in center of bloom. Nonrecurrent, but spring show is outstanding. 6 to 7 feet. Zones 3–11.

'Mrs. B.R. Cant'
■ *Tea, medium pink, 1901, Cant*
Medium-sized fully double flowers are rich red and silvery rose, tinged with blush at base of each petal. 4 to 6 feet. Zones 7–9.

'Rose de Rescht'
■ *Portland, deep pink, very ancient*
Heavily scented fuchsia-red blooms in small tight clusters on short stems. Color can show signs of purple, and is often paler in hot climates. 2 to 3 feet. Zones 3–10.

Rouge Royale ('MEIkarouz')
■ *Hybrid tea, deep red, 2002, Meilland*
Very full quartered burgundy blooms on long stems. From the Romantica series. Extremely fragrant. 3 to 4 feet. Zones 5–9.

Golden Celebration ('AUSgold')
■ *Shrub, deep yellow, 1993, Austin*
Large blooms are more golden than yellow. Flowers are fully double (40+ petals) with concentric rings of broad petals opening to inner golden centers. Blooms—in clusters on strong straight stems—have a

strong rose fragrance. Rain can gather in center of blooms and weigh down even the strongest stem. Plant grows upright 5 to 8 feet tall with dark green foliage. Zones 4 through 10.

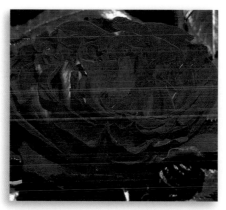

Traviata ('MEllavia')
■ *Hybrid tea, deep red, 1998, Meilland*
One of the new-generation hybrid teas. Very full blooms (100 petals), one to a stem, are vibrant ruby red with a true quartered form reminiscent of old garden roses. The lightly fragrant flowers last for weeks in the vase. Plants are bushy, 4 to 5 feet tall, with lush, highly disease-resistant, dark green foliage. Zones 5 through 10.

Leonardo da Vinci ('MEIdeauri')
■ *Floribunda, medium pink, 1994, Meilland*
Flowers (25 to 30 petals) have the quartered and quilled form of old-fashioned roses. Fragrance is sweet and penetrating. The flowers can withstand rain and wind without severe damage. Plant grows 3 to 4 feet tall, densely covered with medium green foliage. Zones 5 through 10.

Easiest Roses for Splendid Fragrance

The legendary fragrance of roses is one of gardening's greatest joys. That sweet, rosy scent has many variations, from spicy to apple to citrus and clove. The dynamics of fragrance also vary according to the variety—from completely absent to light, medium, or even cloying.

Old garden roses are often masterpieces of fragrance. New breeding trends emphasize scent, although many modern rose breeders still concentrate on achieving ideal form, color, and habit at the expense of fragrance.

It's best to experience a highly fragrant bouquet away from food, because some foods have odors that conflict with the aroma of roses. Bedrooms, bathrooms, closets, hallways, living rooms, and family rooms all benefit from the fragrance of roses.

Longer lasting than the short-lived scent of fresh flowers is rose potpourri. To make potpourri, pick enough roses to fill a 1-quart container with petals. (You can also pick some decorative buds for drying to beautify the finished mix.) Collect the flowers after the dew has dried—around midday. Select just-opened flowers. The more mature the blossom, the less the scent. Dry the petals by spreading them in a single layer on a raised screen in a dark, dry, airy room. Dry them until the petals crunch when squeezed.

Combine the dried petals and a few dried cloves with some dried lavender flowers or other aromatic herbs. In a separate bowl mix 1 tablespoon of orrisroot powder (a fixative) with ground cinnamon and allspice or ground cloves. Add several drops of rose oil and a bit of lavender oil to the spices. Add the spices to the petals and mix again. Store the potpourri in a tightly sealed container in a dark place for a month or more. When the potpourri is ready, you can put it in a dish adorned with dried rosebuds and other dried flowers. The more you keep the dish covered, the longer the scent will last. When you uncover it stir the potpourri to release its fragrance.

'Crimson Glory'
■ *Hybrid tea, dark red, 1935, Kordes*
Though introduced in 1935, this plant has stamina and vigor equal to hybrid teas bred much later in the 20th century. Deep velvety crimson blooms with a pronounced damask fragrance on straight stems. Flowers have about 30 symmetrically arranged petals. Plant is a vigorous, slightly spreading bush with leathery dark green foliage. 4 to 6 feet. Zones 5 through 9.

Constance Spry ('AUSfirst')
■ *Shrub, light pink, 1961, Austin*
Double cup-shaped blooms are a luminous soft pink and exude the delightful fragrance of myrrh. Plant is rather rampant and sprawling, reaching 4 to 8 feet tall and just as wide if not wider. It is often grown as a climber or against a wall to display its best properties. This is not a true repeat-flowering rose, but the bloom cycle is long, stretching well into the summer months. Zones 4 through 9.

MORE EASY ROSES FOR SPLENDID FRAGRANCE

'Chrysler Imperial'
■ *Hybrid tea, dark red, 1952, Lammerts, AARS*
Crimson red blooms (45 petals) with classic, high-centered form, one to a stem. Pronounced fragrance. 4 to 6 feet. Zones 5–9. (Photo page 91.)

Fragrant Plum ('AROplumi')
■ *Grandiflora, mauve, 1990, Christensen*
Lavender blooms age gracefully to smoky plum-purple toward edges. Fragrance is strong and fruity. 4 to 6 feet. Zones 5–10.

Gertrude Jekyll ('AUSbord')
■ *Shrub, medium pink, 1986, Austin*
Large, full-petaled deep pink blooms with a sweet scent. Bush has a lanky habit. 5 to 6 feet. Zones 5–10. (Photo page 51.)

'Henry Hudson'
■ *Hybrid rugosa, white, 1976, Svejda*
Double white flowers with hint of pink at tip of petals. Good fragrance. 3 to 4 feet. Extremely hardy. Zones 2–9.

Iceberg ('KORbin')
■ *Floribunda, white, 1958, Kordes*
Small clusters of fragrant double blooms on well-rounded bush. 3 to 4 feet. Zones 5–10. (Photos pages 9, 32.)

'Ispahan'
■ *Damask, medium pink, before 1832*
Double flowers are consistently bright clear pink with a powerful old-rose fragrance. 4 to 6 feet. Zones 3–9.

'Jens Munk'
■ *Hybrid rugosa, medium pink, 1974, Svejda*
Semidouble soft pink flowers with just a hint of lilac. Handsome yellow and golden stamens. 5 to 6 feet. Zones 2–9.

'Louise Odier'
■ *Bourbon, deep pink, 1851, Margottin*
Very full cupped flowers of warm pink color and rich perfume. 6 to 8 feet. Zones 4–9.

'Mme Alfred Carriere'
■ *Noisette, white, 1879, Schwartz*
Large, globular, pale pinkish-white blooms with just a touch of yellow at base of each petal. 5 to 6 feet. Zones 4–10.

'Roseraie de L'Hay'
■ *Hybrid rugosa, dark red, 1901, Cochet-Cochet*
Big open flowers, crimson-purple with creamy white stamens. Distinct fragrance of cloves and honey. 5 to 6 feet. Zones 4–9.

Fragrant Cloud ('TANellis')
■ *Hybrid tea, orange-red, 1967, Tantau*
Exceptional vigor and bloom production allow frequent cutting. Well-known for heavy perfume. Highly symmetrical flowers (about 30 petals) are nonfading in heat and rain. Large glossy green leaves. Bush can suffer from black spot in damp climates. 3 to 5 feet. Zones 4 through 10.

Sheila's Perfume ('HARsherry')
■ *Floribunda, yellow blend, 1982, Sheridan*
Extremely strong rose-and-fruit scent. The blooms (25 petals) are yellow brushed by deep pink and resemble hybrid teas in size and form. Heavily scented flowers, in small clusters, become larger with more intense color in cool climates. The blooms are weatherproof through rain and heat. Well-rounded 3- to 4-foot-tall plant is loaded with blooms, some as clusters, some as one bloom per stem. Foliage exceptionally glossy green and profuse. Ideal as border plant. Zones 5 through 11.

'Mme Isaac Pereire'
■ *Bourbon, deep pink, 1881, Garcon*
Famous among old garden roses. Huge, full, richly fragrant blooms are deep rose-pink and usually appear in sprays. In autumn, blooms develop purple tint. Flower form is sometimes cupped, sometimes quartered, depending on climate. Exceptionally vigorous plant grows to 7 feet tall. Canes can either be pegged down or trained as climbers to achieve maximum bloom production. Best in warm climates. Zones 5 through 10.

The Ortho Rose Problem Solver

Plant the disease-resistant varieties featured in this book that are hardy in your climate, keep them vigorous with good gardening practices such as regular watering and feeding, and chances are excellent that you will enjoy a lifetime of healthy, colorful roses with few serious problems. Yet periods of drought and inattention are sometimes difficult to avoid, and they can pave the way for disease. And even the most disease-resistant rose can suffer damage from insects.

This chapter will help you solve the most common problems you might encounter with growing roses. It is based on *The Ortho Problem Solver*, a professional reference tool for solving plant problems. Here you will find the experience of many experts, most of them members of research universities and cooperative extension services of various states.

To use Ortho's Rose Problem Solver, first select the picture that looks most like your problem. The map under the photograph shows how likely the problem is to affect your part of North America. If your region is red, the problem is common or severe. If it is yellow, the problem is occasional or moderate. If it is white, the problem is absent or minor.

The problem section describes the symptom or symptoms. The analysis section describes the organisms or cultural conditions causing the problem. The solution section tells you what you can do immediately to alleviate the problem. Then it tells you what changes you can make in the environment or in your gardening practices to prevent the problem from returning.

When you use chemical sprays make certain that roses are listed on the product label. Always read pesticide labels carefully and follow label directions to the letter.

FEW OR NO BLOOMS

Lack of flowers caused by poor pruning.

Rose failing to bloom.

Problem: Plants fail to bloom or bloom only sparsely.

Analysis: Roses produce few or no buds or flowers for any of several reasons.

Solution: The numbered solutions below refer to the numbered items in the analysis.

1. Too much shade: Roses grow and bloom best in full sun. They need at least 4 to 5 hours of direct sunlight for normal blooming.

1. Thin out shading trees and shrubs, or transplant roses to a sunnier location. Replace them with shade-loving plants.

2. Improper dormant pruning: Most rose varieties are grafted onto a rootstock. Tree roses and some climbing roses are grafted onto an intermediate trunkstock. If the hybrid canes are pruned off below the bud union, the rootstock or trunkstock will produce suckers that are flowerless or that produce flowers very different from the desired variety. Some climbing roses and many old-fashioned roses bloom from flower buds formed the previous season. Heavy pruning of such plants will remove all the buds.

2. Do not prune roses below the bud union. Take special care when pruning climbing roses and standard tree roses since the bud union between the trunkstock and the grafted variety may be several feet from the ground. Prune old-fashioned roses lightly during the dormant season. If heavy pruning is needed, wait until after the plants have bloomed in spring.

3. Excessive or improper pruning during the growing season: If roses are excessively trimmed and pruned during the growing season, many or all of the developing flower buds may be inadvertently removed.

3. During the growing season prune roses only to shape them or to remove suckers and dead or dying growth. When cutting or removing flowers, leave at least two 5-leaflet leaves on the cane to ensure continued flower production.

4. Old flowers left on plant: Roses do not produce as many new flowers when the old blooms are allowed to fade and form seeds.

4. Remove flowers as they begin to fade.

5. Flushes of bloom: Many roses bloom in flushes. The first flush usually occurs in late spring, and the second flush occurs in late summer or early fall.

5. You cannot do anything to alter flushes; this is a natural plant cycle.

6. Diseased or infested plants: Roses that have been attacked by diseases or insects do not flower well.

6. Look up the symptoms on the following pages to determine the cause. Treat accordingly.

FLOWER THRIPS

Flower thrips damage.

Problem: Young leaves are distorted, and foliage may be flecked with yellow. Flower buds are deformed and usually fail to open. The petals of open blossoms, especially those of white or light-colored varieties, are often covered with brown streaks and red spots. If a deformed or streaked flower is pulled apart and shaken over white paper, tiny yellow or brown insects fall out and are easily seen against a white background.

Analysis: Flower thrips (*Frankliniella tritici*) are the most abundant and widely distributed thrips in the country. They live inside the buds and flowers of many garden plants. Both the immature and the adult thrips feed on plant sap by rasping the tissue. The injured petal tissue turns brown, and the young expanding leaves become deformed. Injured flower buds usually fail to open. Thrips initially breed on grasses and weeds. When these plants begin to dry up or are harvested, the insects migrate to succulent green ornamental plants. The adults lay their eggs by inserting them into the plant tissue. A complete life cycle may occur in 2 weeks, so populations can build up rapidly. Most damage to roses occurs in early summer.

Solution: Thrips are difficult to control because they continuously migrate to roses from other plants. Immediately remove and destroy infested buds and blooms. Spray with ORTHO Orthene Systemic Insect Control or ORTHO Isotox Insect Killer three times at intervals of 7 to 10 days.

BLACK SPOT

Black spot.

Problem: Circular black spots with fringed margins appear on the upper surfaces of the leaves in the spring. The tissue around the spots or the entire leaf may turn yellow, and the infected leaves may drop prematurely. Severely infected plants may lose all of their leaves by midsummer. Flower production is often reduced, and quality is poor.

Analysis: Black spot is caused by a fungus (*Diplocarpon rosae*) that is a severe problem in areas where high humidity or rain is common in spring and summer. The fungus spends the winter on infected leaves and canes. The spores are spread from plant to plant by splashing water and rain. The fungus enters the tissue, forming spots the size of a pinhead. The black spots enlarge, up to ¾ inch in diameter, as the fungus spreads; spots may join to form blotches. Twigs may also be infected. Plants are often killed by repeated infection.

Solution: Spray with ORTHO RosePride Funginex Rose & Shrub Disease Control, ORTHO RosePride Orthenex Insect & Disease Control, or ORTHO Multi-Purpose Fungicide Daconil 2787® Plant Disease Control. Repeat the treatment at intervals of 7 to 10 days for as long as the weather remains wet. Spraying may be omitted during hot, dry spells in summer. Prune off infected canes. Avoid overhead watering. In the fall, rake up and destroy the fallen leaves. After pruning plants during the dormant season, spray with ORTHO Dormant Disease Control Lime-Sulfur Spray. The following spring, when new growth starts, begin the spray program again. Plant resistant varieties.

POWDERY MILDEW

Powdery mildew.

Problem: Young leaves, young twigs, and flower buds are covered with a thin layer of grayish white powdery material. Infected leaves may be distorted and curled, and many may turn yellow or purplish and drop off. New growth is often stunted, and young canes may be killed. Badly infected flower buds do not open properly. In late summer tiny black dots (spore-producing bodies) may be scattered over the powdery covering like ground pepper.

Analysis: Powdery mildew is caused by a fungus (*Sphaerotheca pannosa* var. *rosae*). It is one of the most widespread and serious diseases of roses. The powdery covering consists of fungal strands and spores. The spores are spread by the wind to healthy plants. The fungus saps plant nutrients, causing distortion, discoloration, and often death of the leaves and canes. Powdery mildew may occur on roses any time during the growing season when rainfall is low or absent, temperatures are between 70 and 80 degrees F, nighttime relative humidity is high, and daytime relative humidity is low. In areas where there is high rainfall in spring and summer, control may not be needed until the drier months of late summer. Rose varieties differ in their susceptibility to powdery mildew.

Solution: Apply ORTHO RosePride Funginex Rose & Shrub Disease Control or ORTHO RosePride Orthenex Insect & Disease Control at the first sign of mildew. Repeat the spray at intervals of 7 to 10 days if mildew reappears. Rake up and destroy leaves in the fall. Plant resistant varieties.

PROBLEM SOLVER
continued

RUST

Rust on rose foliage.

Problem: Yellow to brown spots, up to ¼ inch in diameter, appear on the upper surfaces of leaves, starting in the spring or late fall. The lower leaves are affected first. On the undersides of leaves are spots or blotches containing a red, orange, or black powdery material that can be scraped off. Infected leaves may become twisted and dry and drop off the plant, or they may remain attached. Twigs may also be infected. Severely infected plants lack vigor.

Analysis: Rose rust is caused by any of several species of fungi (*Phragmidium* species) that infest only rose plants. Rose varieties differ in their susceptibility to rust. Wind spreads the orange fungal spores to rose leaves. With moisture (rain, dew, or fog) and moderate temperatures (55 degrees to 75 degrees F), the spores enter the tissue on the undersides of leaves. Spots develop directly above, on the upper surfaces. In the fall, black spores develop in the spots. These spores can survive the winter on dead leaves. In spring, the fungus produces the spores that cause new infections. Rust may also infect and damage young twigs.

Solution: At the first sign of rust, pick off and destroy the infected leaves and spray with ORTHO RosePride Funginex Rose & Shrub Disease Control or ORTHO RosePride Orthenex Insect & Disease Control. Repeat at intervals of 7 to 14 days for as long as conditions remain favorable for infection. Rake up and destroy infected leaves in the fall. Prune off and destroy infected twigs. Apply ORTHO Dormant Disease Control Lime-Sulfur Spray during the dormant season. Plant resistant varieties.

SPIDER MITES

Spider mite damage and webbing.

Problem: Leaves are stippled, bronzed, and dirty. A silken webbing may be found on the lower surfaces of the leaves or on new growth. Infested leaves often turn brown, curl, and drop off. New leaves may be distorted. Plants are usually weak and appear spindly. To determine if a plant is infested with mites, examine the bottoms of the leaves with a hand lens. Or hold a sheet of white paper underneath an affected leaf and tap the leaf sharply. Minute specks the size of pepper grains will drop to the paper and begin to crawl around. The pests are easily seen against the white background.

Analysis: Spider mites, related to spiders, are major pests of many garden and greenhouse plants. They cause damage by sucking sap from the undersides of leaves. As a result of their feeding, the plant's green leaf pigment disappears, producing the stippled appearance. Spider mite webbing traps cast-off skins and debris, making the plant messy. Many leaves may drop off. Severely infested plants produce few flowers. Mites are active throughout the growing season but they thrive in hot, dry weather (70 degrees F and up). By midsummer they can build to tremendous numbers.

Solution: Spray with ORTHO RosePride Orthenex Insect & Disease Control or ORTHO Isotox Insect Killer when damage is first noticed. Cover the undersides of the leaves thoroughly. Repeat the application two more times at intervals of 7 to 10 days.

ROSE LEAFHOPPER

Damaged leaf. Inset: Leafhopper (2× life size).

Problem: Whitish insects, up to ½ inch long, hop and fly away quickly when the plant is touched. The leaves are stippled white. Severely infested plants may be killed.

Analysis: The rose leafhopper (*Edwardsiana rosae*) is a serious pest of roses and apples and infests several ornamental trees as well. It spends the winter as an egg, usually in pimplelike spots on rose canes or on apple bark. When the weather warms in the spring, young leafhoppers emerge and settle on the undersides of leaves. They feed by sucking out the plant sap, which causes the stippling of the leaves. The insects mature, and the females produce a second generation of leafhoppers. Eggs may be deposited in the leaf veins or leaf stems of the rose, or the leafhopper may fly to another woody plant to lay her eggs. This second generation of leafhoppers feeds until fall. By feeding on the leaves and laying eggs in the rose canes, they may kill the plant.

Solution: Spray with ORTHO RosePride Orthenex Insect & Disease Control or ORTHO Rose & Flower Insect Killer when damage is first noticed. Cover the lower surfaces of leaves thoroughly. Repeat the spray if the plant becomes reinfested.

ROSE MIDGE

Rose midge damage.

Problem: The buds are deformed, or black and crisp, and stem tips are dead. This condition develops rapidly. Tiny whitish maggots may be seen feeding at the base of buds or on the stem tips.

Analysis: The rose midge (*Dasineura rhodophaga*) is the larva of a tiny (¹⁄₂₀-inch), yellowish fly that appears in mid- or late summer. The females lay their eggs in the growing tips, flower buds, and unfolding leaves, often twenty or thirty eggs to a bud. The eggs hatch in about 2 days, and the maggots feed, causing the tissue and buds to become distorted and blackened. When mature, the larvae drop to the ground to pupate. New adults appear in 5 to 7 days to lay more eggs. When infestations are severe, most or all of the buds and new shoots in an entire rose garden are killed.

Solution: Cut out and destroy infested stem tips and buds, and spray with ORTHO Orthene Systemic Insect Control. Repeat the spray if the plant becomes reinfested.

VIRUSES

Virus disease in rose.

Problem: Yellow or brown rings, or yellow splotches of various sizes, appear on the leaves. The uninfected portions remain dark green. New leaves may be puckered and curling; flower buds may be malformed. Sometimes there are brown rings on the canes. The plants are usually stunted.

Analysis: Several viruses infect roses. The viruses are transmitted when an infected plant is grafted or budded to a healthy one. This generally occurs in the nursery where the plant is grown. Some plants may show symptoms in only a few leaves. The virus lives throughout the plant, however, and further symptoms may appear later. Most rose viruses are fairly harmless unless there is extensive yellowing or browning. The virus suppresses the development of chlorophyll, causing the splotches or rings. Food production is reduced, which may result in stunted plant growth.

Solution: No cure is available for virus-infected plants. Rose viruses rarely spread naturally; therefore, only weak plants need to be removed. When purchasing rose bushes buy only healthy plants from a reputable dealer.

ROSE APHID

Rose aphids (8× life size).

Problem: Tiny (¹⁄₈-inch), green or pink, soft-bodied insects cluster on leaves, stems, and developing buds. When insects are numerous, flower buds are usually deformed and may fail to open properly. A shiny, sticky substance often coats the leaves. A black, sooty mold may grow on the sticky substance. Ants may be present.

Analysis: Rose aphids (*Macrosiphum rosae*) do little damage in small numbers. Plants can tolerate fairly high populations without much effect. The aphids are extremely prolific, however, and populations can rapidly build to damaging numbers during the growing season. Damage occurs when the aphid sucks the juices from the rose stems and buds. The aphid is unable to digest fully all the sugar in the plant sap and excretes the excess in a fluid called honeydew, which often drops onto the leaves below. A sooty mold may develop on the honeydew, causing the rose plants to appear black and dirty. Ants feed on the sticky substance and are often present where there is an aphid infestation. When aphid populations are high, flower quality and quantity are reduced.

Solution: Spray with ORTHO Isotox Insect Killer, ORTHO Rose & Flower Insect Killer, or an insecticidal soap when clusters of aphids are noticed. Repeat the treatment if the plant becomes reinfested.

PROBLEM SOLVER
continued

LEAFCUTTER BEES

Leafcutter bee damage.

Problem: Small precise ovals or circles are cut from the leaves. Rose twigs with broken or cut ends may die back for several inches. Hairy, black or metallic blue, green, or purple bees are sometimes seen flying around the plant.

Analysis: Leafcutter bees (*Megachile* species) are important pollinators of plants such as alfalfa, clover, and forage crops. The females cut circular pieces of leaf tissue from rose plants to line their nests and plug their egg cells. They usually make their nests in dead rose twigs or other plant twigs that accumulate in the garden. Sometimes they nest in the ends of dying or dead rose stems still attached to the plant. Damage to rose plants is minor.

Solution: Cut out dead and dying stems. Remove dead twigs and plant debris. Since leafcutter bees are pollinators, no chemical controls should be used.

LEAFROLLERS

Rolled leaves.

Problem: Leaves are rolled, usually lengthwise, and tied together with webbing. The rolled leaves are chewed, and the plant may be defoliated. When a rolled leaf is opened, a green caterpillar, ½ to ¾ inch long, may be found inside, surrounded by silky webbing. Flower buds also may be chewed.

Analysis: Several different leafrollers feed on rose leaves and buds. They may also feed on many other plants in the garden. Leafrollers are the larvae of small (up to ¾-inch) brownish moths. The larvae feed on young foliage in the spring, sometimes tunneling into and mining the leaf first. They roll one to several leaves around themselves, tying the leaves together with silken webbing. The leafrollers feed very little once the leaves are rolled. The rolled leaves provide protection from weather, parasites, and chemical sprays. Some leafrollers mature in summer and have several generations during the growing season. Other leafrollers have only one generation per year.

Solution: Spray with ORTHO Orthene Systemic Insect Control or the bacterial insecticide *Bacillus thuringiensis* (Bt) in the spring when leaf damage is first noticed. For the insecticide to be most effective, it should be applied before larvae are protected inside the rolled leaves. Check the plant periodically in spring for the first sign of infestation.

CATERPILLARS

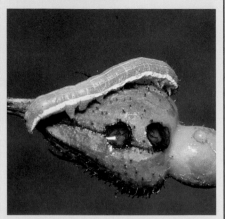

Beet armyworm (life size).

Problem: Holes appear in the leaves and buds. Leaves, buds, and flowers may be entirely chewed off. Worms or caterpillars are feeding on the plants.

Analysis: Many species of these moth or butterfly larvae feed on roses and other garden plants. The adult moths or butterflies of most species start to lay their eggs on garden plants with the onset of warm spring weather. The larvae that emerge from these eggs feed on the leaves, flowers, and buds for 2 to 6 weeks, then pupate in cocoons attached to leaves or structures or buried in the soil. Adult moths and butterflies emerge the following spring.

Solution: Spray infested plants with ORTHO Orthene Systemic Insect Control. The bacterial insecticide *Bacillus thuringiensis* (Bt) may also be used to control caterpillars, especially when they are small.

ROSESLUG

Roseslugs (life size).

Problem: The upper or lower surfaces of leaves are eaten between the veins; the lacy, translucent layer of tissue that remains turns brown. Later, large holes or the entire leaf, except the main vein, may be chewed. Pale green to metallic green sluglike worms, up to ¾ inch long, with large brown heads, may be found feeding on the leaves. Some have hairs covering their bodies, and others appear wet and slimy.

Analysis: Roseslugs are the larvae of black-and-yellow wasps called *sawflies*. The adult wasps appear in spring. They lay their eggs between the upper and lower surfaces of leaves along the leaf edges, with a sawlike egg-laying organ. Depending on the species of sawfly, some of the larvae that emerge exude a slimy substance, giving them a sluglike appearance. Others are hairy. The roseslugs begin feeding on one surface of the leaf tissue, skeletonizing it. Later, several species chew holes in the leaf or devour it entirely. When they are mature the larvae drop to the ground, burrow into the soil, and construct cells in which to pass the winter. Some roseslugs pupate, emerge as sawflies, and repeat the cycle two to six times during the growing season. Severely infested roses may be greatly weakened and produce fewer blooms.

Solution: Spray with an insecticide containing *acephate* or *carbaryl* when damage is first noticed. Repeat as necessary if the rose becomes reinfested.

SCALES

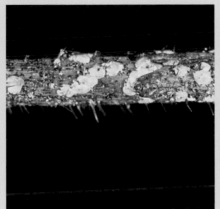

Rose scale (life size).

Problem: White, cottony masses; brown or black crusty bumps; or clusters of somewhat flattened white, yellowish, or brown scaly bumps cover the stems and leaves. The bumps can be scraped or picked off. Leaves turn yellow and may drop. In some cases a shiny, sticky substance coats the leaves. A black, sooty mold often grows on the sticky substance. Heavy infestations kill the stems.

Analysis: Many different types of scales infest roses. They lay their eggs on the leaves or canes, and in spring to midsummer the young scales, called crawlers, settle on the leaves and twigs. These small (¹⁄₁₀-inch), soft-bodied young feed by sucking sap from the plant. The legs usually atrophy, and with some types, a shell develops over the body. The types of scales that do not develop shells are conspicuous. Females of the cottony cushion scale are covered with a white cottony egg sac containing up to 2,500 eggs. Scales covered with a shell are less noticeable. Their shell often blends in with the plant, and the eggs are inconspicuous beneath their covering. Some species of scales are unable to digest fully all the sugar in the plant sap, and they excrete the excess in a fluid called honeydew.

Solution: Control with ORTHO Isotox Insect Killer or ORTHO Orthene Systemic Insect Control when the young are active. To control overwintering insects, treat with ORTHO Volck Oil Spray in the spring.

BEETLES

Fuller rose beetle (4× life size).

Problem: Holes appear in the flowers and flower buds; open flowers may be entirely eaten. Often affected buds fail to open, or they open deformed. Stem tips may be chewed, or the leaves may be notched or riddled with holes. Red, green-spotted, brownish, or metallic green beetles up to ½ inch long are sometimes seen on the flowers or foliage.

Analysis: Several types of beetles infest roses. They may destroy the ornamental value of the plant by seriously damaging the flowers and foliage. The insects usually spend the winter as larvae in the soil or as adults in plant debris on the ground. In late spring or summer, mature beetles fly to roses and feed on the flowers, buds, and sometimes leaves. Punctured flower buds usually fail to open, and flowers that do open are often devoured. Many beetles feed at night, so their damage may be all that is noticed. Female beetles lay their eggs in the soil or in flowers in late summer or fall. The emerging larvae crawl down into the soil to spend the winter, or they mature and pass the winter as adults. The larvae of some beetles feed on plant roots before maturing in the fall or spring.

Solution: Spray with ORTHO Isotox Insect Killer or ORTHO Orthene Systemic Insect Control when damage is first noticed. Repeat the spray if the rose becomes reinfested.

PROBLEM SOLVER
continued

CROWN GALL

Crown gall appearing at the base of a plant.

Problem: Large corky galls up to several inches in diameter appear at the base of the plant and on the stems and roots. The galls are rounded, with rough, irregular surfaces, and may be dark and cracked. Plants with numerous galls are weak; growth is slowed and leaves turn yellow. Branches or the entire plant may die back. Plants with only a few galls often show no other symptoms, however.

Analysis: Crown gall is caused by a soil-inhabiting bacterium (*Agrobacterium tumefaciens*) that infects many ornamentals and fruit trees in the garden. The bacteria are often brought to a garden initially on the stems or roots of an infected plant and are spread with the soil and contaminated pruning tools. The bacteria enter the plant through wounds in the roots or the stem. They produce a compound that stimulates rapid cell growth in the plant, causing gall formation on the roots, crown, and sometimes branches. The galls may disrupt the flow of water and nutrients up the roots and stems, weakening and stunting the top of the plant. Galls do not usually cause the death of the plant.

Solution: Crown gall cannot be eliminated from a plant. An infected plant may survive for many years, however. To improve its appearance, prune out and destroy galled stems. Disinfect pruning shears after each cut by dipping in a solution of 1 part chlorine bleach and 9 parts water. Destroy severely infected plants. The bacteria will remain in the soil for 2 to 3 years. If you wish to replace the infected roses soon, select other plants that are resistant to crown gall.

STEM CANKERS AND DIEBACK

Stem cankers.

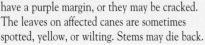

Problem: Yellowish, reddish, or brown sunken areas develop on the canes. The sunken areas may have a purple margin, or they may be cracked. The leaves on affected canes are sometimes spotted, yellow, or wilting. Stems may die back.

Analysis: Several different fungi cause stem cankers on roses, with the *Coniothyrium* species being most common. During wet or humid weather, the fungi enter the plant at a wound caused by the thorns or at a cut stem. A sunken canker develops and expands through the tissue in all directions. The fungus may cut off the flow of nutrients and water through the stem, causing the leaves to wilt or yellow and the twigs to die back. Rose plants that are infected with black spot or in a weakened condition are more susceptible to invasion by stem canker fungi.

Solution: Cut out and destroy cankered canes at least 5 inches below the infected area. Disinfect pruning tools after each cut by dipping in a solution of 9 part water and 1 part chlorine bleach. After pruning, spray the canes with a fungicide containing lime sulfur. Sprays aimed at controlling black spot will help control canker. Or spray with ORTHO Multi-Purpose Fungicide Daconil 2787® Plant Disease Control or a fungicide containing *mancozeb*, starting in the spring. Repeat every 10 to 14 days for as long as the weather is wet or humid. Keep the plants vigorous by feeding, watering, and pruning properly.

BORERS

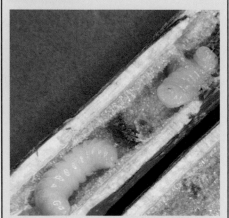

Carpenter bee larvae (3× life size).

Problem: Several or all of the larger canes and stems wilt and die. If the bark is peeled back, or if dying stems are sliced open, white to yellowish worms or legless grubs up to ¾ inch long may be revealed. Affected stems may be swollen at the base.

Analysis: Many kinds of insects bore into rose stems. They include certain sawflies, beetles, horntail wasps, and solitary bees. Some of these attack old, weakened plants or plants that are under stress from recent transplant or improper care; such borers often attack at the base of the plant. Other borers attack healthy rose plants, either traveling in a spiral pattern just under the bark or burrowing down through the center of the rose stems. Most rose borers produce one generation per year.

Solution: Prune out and destroy infested rose stems. Make the cut several inches below the point where the stem is wilted or swollen. If an insect has tunneled a hole through the center of the stem, keep cutting the stem lower to the ground until you find and destroy the insect or see the end of the tunnel. If this is a problem year after year, seal rose canes immediately after pruning with ORTHO Pruning Sealer or with a thumbtack to prevent borers from penetrating the soft tissue in the center of the stem. Keep rose plants in good health.

SELECTED MAIL-ORDER SOURCES

The varieties listed in this book are generally available at your local nursery at bare-root season. The larger companies providing roses wholesale to retail nurseries are Weeks Roses and Jackson & Perkins. Some varieties, however, may require to be purchased via mail order, particularly the varieties mentioned in the sections for hardiness, shrubs, miniatures and old garden roses. The following companies have mail-order catalogs:

MAINLY LARGE ROSES

Arena Rose Company
P.O. Box 3096
525 Pine Street
Paso Robles, CA 93447
888-466-7434
Fax: 888-347-5580
Website: arenaroses.com

Edmunds' Roses
6235 S.W. Kahle Road
Wilsonville, OR 97070
888-481-7673
Fax: 503-682-1275
Website: edmundsroses.com
E-mail: info@edmundsroses.com

Jackson & Perkins
1 Rose Lane
P.O. Box 1028
Medford, Oregon 97501
800-292-4769
Fax: 800-242-0329
Website: jacksonandperkins.com

Johnny Becnel Show Roses, Inc.
8910 Highway 23
Belle Chasse, LA 70037
504-394-6608

Wayside Gardens
1 Garden Lane
Hodges, SC 29695
800-845-1124
Website: waysidegardens.com

OLD GARDEN ROSES

Heirloom Roses
24062 N.E. Riverside Drive
St. Paul, OR 97137
503-538-1576
Fax: 503-538-5902
Website: heirloomroses.com

Pickering Nurseries, Inc.
670 Kingston Road
Pickering, Ontario
Canada L1V 1A6
905-839-2111
Fax: 905-839-4807
Website: pickeringnurseries.com

Vintage Gardens Antique Roses
2833 Old Gravenstein Highway
   South
Sebastopol, CA 95472
707-829-2035
Fax: 707-829-9516
Website: vintagegardens.com

MINIATURE ROSES

Bridges Roses
2734 Toney Road
Lawndale, NC 28090
704-538-9412
Fax: 704-538-1521
Website: bridgesroses.com

Michael's Premier Roses
9759 Elder Creek Road
Sacramento, CA 95829
916-369-7673
Fax: 916-361-1141
Website: michaelsrose.com
E-mail: michael@michaelsrose.com

Mitchie's Rose and More
830 S. 373rd Street
Federal Way, WA 98003
253-815-1072
The Mini Rose Garden
P.O. Box 203
Cross Hill, SC 29332
864-998-4331
888-998-2424
Website: minirosegarden.com

Nor'East Miniature Roses, Inc.
P.O. Box 307
58 Hammond Street
Rowley, MA 01969
800-426-6485
Website: noreast-miniroses.com
E-mail: nemr@shore.net

Rosemania
4020 Trail Ridge Drive
Franklin, TN 37067
888-600-9665
Fax: 615-790-4981
Website: rosemania.com

Sequoia Nursery
2519 East Noble Avenue
Visalia, CA 93292
559-732-0309
Website: miniatureroses.com/moore

Taylor's Roses
P.O. Box 677
Fairhope, AL 36533
251-928-5008
Email: taylorsroses@earthlink.net

Tiny Petals Mini Rose Nursery
489 Minot Avenue
Chula Vista, CA 91910
619-498-4755
Fax: 619-422-0385
Website: tinypetalsnursery.com

Top left: 'Chrysler Imperial' (hybrid tea)
Bottom left: X-Rated (miniature)

USDA Plant Hardiness Zone Map

This map of climate zones helps you select plants for your garden that will survive a typical winter in your region. The United States Department of Agriculture (USDA) developed the map, basing the zones on the lowest recorded temperatures across North America. Zone 1 is the coldest area and Zone 11 is the warmest.

Plants are classified by the coldest temperature and zone they can endure. For example, plants hardy to Zone 6 survive where winter temperatures drop to –10° F. Those hardy to Zone 8 die long before it's that cold. These plants may grow in colder regions but must be replaced each year. Plants rated for a range of hardiness zones can usually survive winter in the coldest region as well as tolerate the summer heat of the warmest one.

To find your hardiness zone, note the approximate location of your community on the map, then match the color band marking that area to the key.

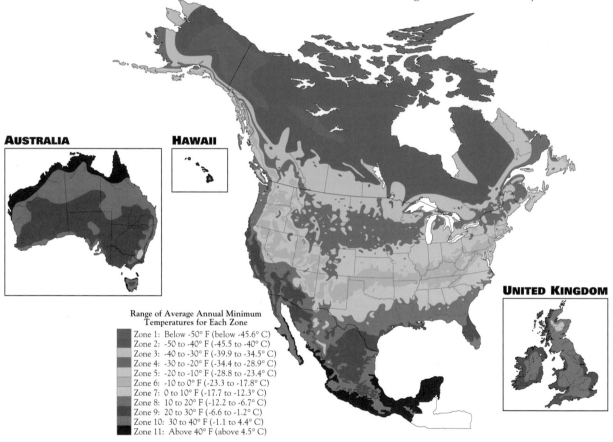

AUSTRALIA

HAWAII

UNITED KINGDOM

Range of Average Annual Minimum Temperatures for Each Zone

Zone 1: Below -50° F (below -45.6° C)
Zone 2: -50 to -40° F (-45.5 to -40° C)
Zone 3: -40 to -30° F (-39.9 to -34.5° C)
Zone 4: -30 to -20° F (-34.4 to -28.9° C)
Zone 5: -20 to -10° F (-28.8 to -23.4° C)
Zone 6: -10 to 0° F (-23.3 to -17.8° C)
Zone 7: 0 to 10° F (-17.7 to -12.3° C)
Zone 8: 10 to 20° F (-12.2 to -6.7° C)
Zone 9: 20 to 30° F (-6.6 to -1.2° C)
Zone 10: 30 to 40° F (-1.1 to 4.4° C)
Zone 11: Above 40° F (above 4.5° C)

METRIC CONVERSIONS

U.S. Units to Metric Equivalents			Metric Units to U.S. Equivalents		
To Convert From	Multiply By	To Get	To Convert From	Multiply By	To Get
Inches	25.4	Millimeters	Millimeters	0.0394	Inches
Inches	2.54	Centimeters	Centimeters	0.3937	Inches
Feet	30.48	Centimeters	Centimeters	0.0328	Feet
Feet	0.3048	Meters	Meters	3.2808	Feet
Yards	0.9144	Meters	Meters	1.0936	Yards

To convert from degrees Fahrenheit (F) to degrees Celsius (C), first subtract 32, then multiply by $\frac{5}{9}$.

To convert from degrees Celsius to degrees Fahrenheit, multiply by $\frac{9}{5}$, then add 32.

INDEX

Note: Page numbers in **bold** indicate photographs and illustrations.

ROSE INDEX

GENERAL INDEX